HOW TO BE A
SUCCESSFUL
COACH

JAMES B. BONDER, Ed. D.
Line Coach, West Chester State Teachers College, Pa.

HOW TO BE A
SUCCESSFUL
COACH

PRENTICE-HALL, INC.
Englewood Cliffs, N.J.
1958

PRINTED IN THE UNITED STATES OF AMERICA

40220

TO

W. Glenn Killinger

Not only a winning coach but a football institution enshrined forever in the
hearts of his men.

PREFACE

The book is the result of 25 years of coaching experience that have completely monopolized the author's interest. This has been augmented by knowledge absorbed from fellow coaches and from rich experiences resulting from the attendance at numerous football clinics and meetings.

The text is designed primarily to strengthen those facets of the game which have been overlooked. A decade ago coaches needed only to be skilled in imparting to their players the mechanical techniques of the sport. Today athletics no longer belong solely to the players and coaches. Part of its management has been usurped by the fans at large. This condition has necessitated the understanding and development of varied relationships that directly affect players and coaches.

The author's purpose in writing this book is to familiarize the coach, through an elementary presentation, with the concepts of relationships within the athletic framework.

The entire organization of the book is aimed to train the coach to recognize and understand the many intricate fluctuations in the basic relationships, so that his position will be strengthened. Parents, faculty, press, and community relationships are emphasized because each becomes a necessary ingredient in the emergence of a stronger coach-player kinship.

Techniques are presented to show how a healthy and normal relationship can be maintained without losing equilibrium.

The author is conscious of his limitations, aware that there is no best way. It is, however, his hope that all coaches will find the work informative, illuminative, and even provocative.

The preparation of this text would have been impossible without the valuable assistance of many people. The author is especially indebted to Mae Shuey and Dr. Harry Stine, who read the entire manuscript and offered many helpful suggestions and critical comments in the organizational content.

A special thanks to Pat Rhymes, Ruth and Frances Polinowsky, who slaved through a maze of pages to type the original work. A word of gratitude to Mr. Alan Williams, of Prentice-Hall, Inc., who planted the original seed for this book.

Meriting special appreciation are the many coaches, too numerous to mention, whose ingenious ideas over the years contributed indirectly to the undertaking.

JIM BONDER

TABLE OF CONTENTS

A QUASI-AUTOCRATIC RELATIONSHIP

—the basis for a successful season

*The rigid volunteer rules of right and wrong in sports are second only to religion——*HERBERT HOOVER

What will be said in this chapter will be more disturbing than appealing to some; nevertheless, truth must reign.

It is not difficult to recognize the significance of Herbert Hoover's statement. The former president was writing of the rigid volunteer rules which govern our athletic competition. Knute Rockne and, more recently, Jim Tatum compared athletics with ultimate success in war. It is no accident that they proceeded along that line of reasoning, for successful athletics require as strict obedience as does the military.

Autocracy to Democracy

Your relationship to your players finds an unwritten tradition emerging. You are the team's rod and staff. At best it is a quasi-autocratic inter-personal relationship. At times you assume the role of an unyielding, strict, authoritarian tyrant, while on other occasions your willingness to submit to the wishes of the players

1

results in a democratic rule. All successful teams are directed by this peculiar alliance between coaches and players.

As players freely accept this formula, a democratic concept appears in part. As a matter of fact, readers will discover many incidents of popular principles being utilized. The secret is to initiate such procedures without losing control. It involves the skill of dominating without whipping the initiative out of a player.

Coaching is the arrangement of players to achieve a common purpose effectively. It has never been otherwise and will not be unless man develops a creative force nullifying the need for authority. To date, this force seems very, very remote, despite attempted inroads made by pragmatists and educators who have vainly endeavored to introduce a democratic concept into the American sports program. The ugly words, "playing the game for fun," convey athletic schizophrenia to the hearts of successful American tutors. Men in the field who change techniques merely to be in fashion have learned early the folly of this undertaking. Can you visualize someone arriving late at the Army-Navy game, or the Baseball All-Star game, and inquiring about the score, only to be stared at with perplexity and disdain. Can you imagine spectators uttering, "Score? Why, they are just playing for the fun of it—no one is keeping score." These misdirected spectators would be awed at the overflow of statistics kept by all teams engaged in major sports.

Every Game a Command Performance

Imagine Yogi Berra saying to Mickey Mantle, "Mickey, I followed you the last time in the batting order. Now let's be democratic and fair—this time you follow me." Picture Casey Stengel inquiring of the grandstand managers whether to bunt or hit away. Years ago, Mr. Veeck, of the St. Louis Browns, by hurriedly taking a consensus of opinions as to the strategy to be employed, permitted the crowd to manage the team. Needless to say, Veeck's club simply lost another game.

Leadership by all leads to leadership for none, and that spells chaos and confusion. If coaching were meant to be a cooperative effort, no coach could be fired, because the fans would have to be discharged with him. The price a coach pays is the right of those who surrender their thinking to him to fire him. Criticizing a coach is the perpetual right of the public, because he alone pulls the strings that make the puppets dance.

Picture again Durocher ordering the batter to bunt, and having the hitter ignore it. A fine, suspension, or even retirement to the minors would follow. Try to imagine the confusion of Coach Woody Hayes, of Ohio State, hypothetically instructing his quarterback to punt during the 1954 Rose Bowl game, and having it ignored. Successful coaches permit no exception to instructions coming directly from them. Paul Brown, of the Cleveland Browns, personally calls every play by a system similar in principle to carrier pigeons, with the guards carrying messages.

In athletics, as in war, there cannot be compromise. To be democratic would mean having people lead who have had no training in leadership. You must be secure in your sense of unchallenged authority in order to be a real instrument in your team's success.

A Voluntary Submission

The quasi-autocratic relationship is not a difficult one, for players willingly subscribe to it. It is unique in that probably no other organization in society enjoys this. Players realize and accept without question the necessity for the coach to make all major decisions. It is a willing submission and conformity on the part of players. Whatever players do and however hard they try, they cannot win by tipping the scales of authority in their favor. They can only win by losing gracefully to the authority. They realize success is dependent upon strict obedience. For some unexplainable reason, players do not resent the strictness of these demands. They recognize that belonging to a team means surrendering something. They relinquish their right to individual security in order to share in a collective security. As they are security conscious by nature, the process is a simple one.

To be added to the procedure is the immediate reward every player receives because he belongs to a team. As long as prestige accrues to them, players willingly will humble themselves. This apparent meekness does not diminish the personal relationship of the player and the outside world. If anything, he gains esteem because most players aspire to become coaches. They also obey because that is the only road to earning the right to similar treatment from their own players in the future.

Of course, a thinking coach utilizes the imagination of his players and encourages such enterprise, despite limiting it to the basic tenets he has taught. Imagination and thinking are necessary, but must remain within spheres established through your teaching. Successful coaching implies the developing of a mechanized society which makes every player part of a controlled mass. Young players want to be led and look to their coach as one whose decisions are a major factor in winning. In fact, good coaches spend hours with their charges explaining strategy in detail, and this process enables the players to share in whatever game plan is devised. It is this procedure of detailed planning shared with a squad that enables them to accept decisions at game time without question. Conformity and obedience are necessary qualities to have in your players. They must be mechanical reactions. Instill in your players a desire to be led, an urge to be driven, to be governed, and a yen to be enslaved. It is analogous to a woman's desire to be led by the man she marries.

No Compromise

During the 1947 World Series, Floyd Bevens of the New York Yankees had pitched a no-hit, no-run game for eight-and-two-thirds innings. Only one out away from immortality, Bevens yielded a double to pinch-hitter Cookie Lavagetto, and the next man walked. Individual acclaim and fame gave way to a team concept. Bevens was yanked for a relief pitcher. Manager Harris dared not compromise individual achievement for team success. One's obligation towards team success swallows up and relieves players of their individuality.

Your strength is revealed in hardness. You must stand independent and resist all attempts to be governed by your own or the spectators' emotions. Coaches are the only realists left in this society full of pragmatic "happy planners."

Coaching Is a Hierarchy

Actually, coaching is unlimited despotism. To be democratic means authority reaches from *"down up"* and autocratic from *"top down."* Because coaching is dependent upon tolerant, cöercive forces, it must be autocratic.

As a coach, you cannot be pious or benevolent, for you must obtain results which can be realized only when idealistic thoughts give way to realism. You are constantly working toward thought control. Players are required to think your thoughts, speak your words, and follow your habits. It is a sterile conformity. Players live in a hell of athletic insecurity which is generated by your changing demands, plus your refusal to be pleased, regardless of the effort. Players must develop a capacity for adaptation regardless of the absurd demand. The oddity is that coaches believe, and the players share the assumption, that there cannot be a dissolution of legitimate authority. The functional aspect of that idea rests upon its common acceptance. This dynastic power cannot be dissolved for it is the heart of a strange organization. To alter it would result not in change but in the collapse of all worthwhile athletic achievement. There is validity in the statement, "Honor and obey the coach."

"Give the Game Back to the Players"?

This phrase is repeated year after year, even though it is ludicrous and incapable of being fulfilled. The game can never return to the players, because the players never had it. What coach with any common sense would consent to placing his bread and butter into the hands of a group of inexperienced players? To "give the game back to the players" it would be necessary to re-form the basic concepts of our American athletics. The public would have to be conditioned to ignore victory; anyone could then direct the team. In this era, achieving such an objective would be as difficult as remaining alive yet refusing to breathe. At best, it becomes an ostrich's view of things. We realize the overwhelming task, the futility of trying to minimize victory. Without wins and losses sport loses its basic and intrinsic values. We certainly cannot compromise victory. We can lose gracefully, but in order to accomplish this, someone must win so you can become a gracious loser. If, therefore, winning is still important in athletics, and coaching competency depends on winning, then it is pure folly to intrust the game to players. Imagine players who have had no training in such an undertaking making critical decisions instead of the coaches. The modern pragmatist swears by these principles as the answer to all our problems. However, I would like to pose a question: Is it more democratic if control is taken from the coach and awarded to a player? Someone must hold the reins. Taking them from the coach and passing them to an inexperienced player doesn't make it more democratic. It merely transfers the responsibility. Veterans like John McGraw, Knute Rockne, Miller Huggins, Casey Stengel, Frank Leahy, Hugo Bezdek, and Glenn Killinger, all gallant veterans, would become indignant at the suggestion of utilizing the democratic processes in sports. To them any attempt to vary the "status quo" would not be a change but a *corruption* of the relationship. Our problem today is not a case of freedom *"from what"* but freedom *"for what."* The realistic concept would read "free to do the bidding of the experienced person in charge"—the coach.

Athletics cannot exist unless a controlling power is placed somewhere. Because there is so little from within the players, there must be more from without—namely you, the coach.

Utilizing Parental Help to Strengthen Your Coaching

Utilizing the cooperation of parents requires a technical skill on your part which culminates in no pain being felt by the players. A youngster engaging in athletic competition for the first time is shocked at the drastic new relationship. It differs from any other to which he has been exposed, including those in his own home. To this young boy, the strange man referred to as the coach appears hard-hearted and ruthless. You must establish balance in this youngster's thinking. Call upon the parents explaining that you want to transfer the integrity of the home to your locker room. Parents exercise enormous influence on their children and good tutors must utilize it as a means of establishing good rapport. Parents must be assured that a common bond exists between you, them, and their progeny. Common because you assure them that your interest in their boy is genuine and of a parental nature. Once you have gained the confidence of parents, youngsters will soon follow their example. Every good American home wants to know something about the people in whose hands they place the destinies of their loved ones. Coaches who explain their objectives to parents and the techniques by which they can reach those goals, automatically make them partners, and a cooperative effort results. They now share his unquestionable belief in the game he teaches. Parents are also convincd that athletic characteristics will be woven into the boy's life which will aid in his well-rounded development.

A youngster castigated by a coach for the first time is timid and in doubt. If authority is exercised too strenuously the boy could be lost easily. However, once he realizes that his parents know and approve of you, the boy will accede more readily to the domination.

Coaching Is Player Management

Effective coaching cannot be a function of coaching competence alone. It is also, at the very least, a function of adequate player management, which is an indispensible component of a successful relationship. It is essential to give that phase separate consideration. Outstanding coaches have helped contrive the eight following time-tested tenets of management.

1. Ability to develop an organization.
2. Personal leadership.
3. Ability to plan work.
4. Technical coaching knowledge.
5. Cooperation in executing school policies.

6. Judgment and decisions.
7. Acceptance of responsibilities.
8. Constructive and independent thinking.

Each principle will be taken up separately.

1. Ability to Develop an Organization

A coach's value is proportionate to the usefulness of the players whose efforts he directs. The ability to establish and maintain an effective organization that meets current needs and future changing requirements is essential. The chain of minor league baseball teams and freshmen football squads is sufficient proof of this need.

A coach must check his past judgement in selecting players to fill certain assignments. If performance has measured up to expectations, he has a good rule for the future. If not, ask where the player failed, where you failed, and guard against repeating the mistake. Analyze the performance of your players in order to provide a basis for building a well-balanced, complete organization. Study the aptitudes and abilities of each team member to be sure the talents represented are adaptable to what is required for immediate success. Since requirements do change, you must look ahead to the next game, the next month, and the next season.

2. Personal Coaching Leadership

Personal coaching leadership in developing assistants and players to maximum efficiency, enthusiasm, and teamwork gives a team a punch that produces recognizable results.

So essential is personal leadership to good coaching that some coaches well equipped in this respect have been able to compensate for deficiencies in other factors. The term "leadership," though broad and hard to define, involves selling, planning and teaching. It is necessary to sell yourself to your team; to win both respect and friendship by your actions and attitudes. Plan the team's work in such a way that you are pointing out a path to follow. Teach team members the things they need to know, developing the fullest potential of each. Be everything you expect them to be, in enthusiasm, in loyalty and in hard work.

3. Ability to Plan Work

Fiery enthusiasm in a team is ill-spent unless a coach has the ability to analyze and plan with efficiency every minute spent on the field. Coaches must plan their work in order to know what they wish to accomplish. Good coaching never depends on trial and error. Goals must be established for every player every day. A good plan will substitute thinking for worry. It provides for "ifs" "ands" and "buts." It will simplify activities and save valuable time for more important routines. Interruptions and delays are prevented, for proper planning means work finished on time.

Good coaching is good teaching transferred from the classroom to the field. Plans on the field are made just as meticulously as those in the classroom. As in lesson planning, every good coach must have definite aims and objectives, meet the needs of his players, compensate for individual differences and offer rewards and losses. Planning enables a fast pace to be kept with breaks reduced to a minimum.

It is best to write out your coaching plan, because activity breeds ambition and progress. Put your plan on paper and place it on the bulletin board and you will never be the engineer of a train running from "Nowhere" to "Nowhere." The following items are helpful in planning:

    a. Set up objectives for every player.
    b. Break them down into parts.
    c. Set a time schedule making sure each knows his assignment.
    d. Hold every player responsible for carrying out the plans.
    e. Evaluate the plan.

4. Technical Knowledge in Coaching

Coaches who are lacking in technical knowledge but who insist on working are guilty of committing a cardinal sin. It is most unfair to the players exposed to them. Young people have the right to be led by an enthusiastic, competent coach regardless of circumstances. Coaches must constantly strive to improve their knowledge of their particular game. Old dogs can still learn new tricks. Most games are changing with the advent of professional participation. Try to read the books of, or talk to, outstanding men as often as possible. One half hour a day for a year spent in improving your knowledge is equal in time to 140 hours or three and one half work weeks.

5. Cooperation in Executing School Athletic Policies

All coaches must understand, explain, and secure adherence to a school's policies and suggest procedures for making them more effective. Regardless of whether or not you agree with the rules, make every attempt to carry them out. It is more profitable to make a constructive suggestion than to indulge in futile complaining. The good of the school must be placed above your own selfish and immediate interests. Above all, do not keep your players in the dark. Help them to understand every phase of the school's policy that affects them, then hold them responsible for the policy.

6. Judgment and Decisions

To keep a team clicking smoothly, a coach must exercise sound judgment and make prompt, effective decisions. Some coaches are a game behind, and invariably, they lose. To make quick, sound decisions, a coach must thoroughly know his men and their capacities. He must study those factors from every possible viewpoint. A quick classification and arrangement of all the facts must be made before a complete analysis can be made. Try to test completely, in your own mind, the conclusions reached. Have you allowed personal feeling or preconceived notions to influence your decisions? Always profit by a wrong judgment and do not repeat the error.

7. Acceptance of Responsibility

A coach willingly assumes sole responsibility for team failures and relinquishes all credit for its success to team members and assistants. Be loyal to administrators, but do not be a "yes" man. If two people in an organization always agree, one of them is unnecessary—it could be you. Have a clear-cut, definite outline of your responsibilities, then seek added responsibilities which will make you more valuable to the school.

8. Constructive and Independent Thinking

Thinking independently implies a refusal to be tied down to past or present methods and techniques. Thinking constructively weighs the advantages and disadvantages of departing from established precedents. Constructive thinking is disciplined thinking directed along channels, in order to bring about more effective results. To follow an established pattern simply because it has always been followed is lame reasoning. The coaching profession needs men possessing creative imaginations. Progress feeds on initiative and new ideas. Change, however, merely to be in fashion is as dangerous as building defensory mechanisms to keep out new ideas. Remember, change means work; there cannot be any ingrained inertia in coaching ranks.

Evaluate every new idea through honest critical analysis. This will bring about a reduction of criticism on the part of fellow coaches. There always have been, and always will be, new ideas, otherwise athletics would become degenerate and stagnant. There is no rule in coaching that prevents one from working a new concept into an established practice. Coaches should have conviction in their findings, and above all, the courage for their implimentation.

I have always likened the coach to a court judge. Because the ideal coach exemplifies the ideal judge, the following is appropriate:

> At home he's a man much like the rest of us. He plays with his children, frowns over his bills, reads his newspaper, discusses the weather with the neighbors.

> But in the morning when he goes to work, he puts on a plain black robe and becomes something bigger than himself.

There's a touch of ceremony as he walks into the court-
room. "Please rise," says the Clerk, in a formal kind of
voice. "His Honor, the Judge . . ."

And we all stand for a moment in silence and respect, to
remind His Honor and ourselves of what we expect from a
man we've asked to wear the plain black robe of justice.

Now his difficult work begins. People talk to him—arguers
all; attackers and defenders, each believing that he alone is
right. Feelings run high, voices are raised, tempers are lost,
manners are forgotten—but not by the Judge. He is a
soother of tempers, a referee among fighters, a cool guard-
ian of the rules. He is the protector of both sides, and the
partisan of neither. Both sides hope to sway him, and hope
even more that he cannot be swayed.

What does he think about, sitting high and lonely on the
bench? It is only the law, or is there something else? Maybe
he remembers with some deeper part of his mind, that all
the laws written in his big book are different ways of
saying one simple thing: We, the people want fair play
for every man. Maybe that is what keeps him strong and
clear and calm while the angry arguments swirl around
him.

"Your Honor" we call him. But it is our own honor we
mean. We have woven into the black robe the ideals that
make up the honor of an American—our devotion to what
is right and good.*

A coach must aspire to all the above, and the closer he ap-
proximates the judicial image, the more respect he will receive.
There is another distinct similarity between the judge and the
coach: when either reaches a decision it is accepted because
both are furnished with recognized authority.

Nice Guys Don't Win—Leo Durocher

Never having spoken personally to Leo Durocher, the greatest manager in baseball, it is difficult to interpret accurately his
statement, "Nice guys don't win." The quotation in itself, however, is most challenging and fascinating. No one gains popularity when inflicting frustration upon someone else.

---

* "We call him His Honor to remind us of our own." Reprinted through the
courtesy of the John Hancock Mutual Life Insurance Company.

Every coach creates frustration when he interferes with the natural drives and desires of his charges. One of the reasons a boy submits to the authoritarian will of his coach is because of the reward he receives through participation. There are times when a football coach substitutes and a baseball manager uses a pinch hitter; neither one is popular with the player who is being replaced. To want to play, to have a burning desire to play which is equal to a passion, is a necessary ingredient in a competitor's success. Yet at times, a coach thwarts this desire. When he does, he is not liked. His Trendex rating hits a new low. This dislike soon subsides and a normal relationship replaces it.

Parents who have blocked a child's desire have been hated by their own child. Nevertheless, they were duty bound to guide the child, despite his protestation. The destructive emotions soon subside and are replaced with more constructive feelings. Being liked must not be interpreted as synonymous with being respected. If a coach took the time to consider the respective feelings of his players and their past achievements, and allowed himself to become a sentimentalist, he would lose more often than he won. The coach's thinking must be free from such softness, otherwise he will be receiving sympathy for extensive reverses.

To rely on the strength of past performances, and use a player who at present is incompetent, is unfair to another youngster yearning for an opportunity to break in. Every season is replete with instances where younger players have replaced older stars.

All team players may dislike a coach, but at the same time respect him for his fiery aggression and burning desire to win. "Nice guys don't win" implies not being liked in the immediate present, for coaches making changes are temporarily disliked by the substituted player. On the other hand, "Nice guys do win," if one evaluates the coaching relationship remotely. After players reassess the situation, they invariably think of their coach with feelings of love and admiration. Glenn Killinger, a 1921 All-American and West Chester's outstanding coach, was tutored by Hugo Bezdek, one of the greatest mentors of all time. In 1955 Bezdek lay dying in an Atlantic City hospital and while he drew his last breath, Killinger tearfully held the old man's hand. This exemplifies man's devotion to man.

Some of every coach's qualities have rubbed off on all his players. It makes for immortality. Past dislikes, heartaches, and irritability have compelled players and coaches to learn to understand each other. A sincere friendship develops which persists for years.

The Legend of Knute Rockne—"A Nice Guy"

At a time in our sports history when wrestling has become a farce, basketball has been marked by scandals, football is being investigated, and boxing is at a low ebb, some names come ringing down the corridor of purity and cleanliness to form an inspiring beacon.

The following pages are a eulogy to one of these men, Knute Rockne, whose career gives veracity to the interpretation that, remotely, "Nice guys do win." Rockne was more than a coach; he was an educator and a moulder of men. Some of our young coaches would be wise to emulate his exemplary life. As a coach he went beyond the sphere of just teaching blocking and tackling. He left his players a sense of decency, honor, kindness, affection, and above all, a man to man sense of fellowship which has persisted for generations. Yet the majority of Rockne's players at the time they were attending Notre Dame detested his absolute, monarchical methods. Being chosen mythical national champions for three consecutive years did not ease the rancor. Graduation and leaving the campus, however, soon changed the detestation into respect, admiration, and love.

In March 1931, Rockne was on his way to Hollywood to make a picture depicting his great Notre Dame teams. His plane had made a stop at Kansas City where his sons were attending school. The next morning he wired his vacationing wife, Bonnie, " 'Leaving today—boys fine—love and kisses,'—Knute."

It was a bad morning; the ceiling was low. The plane's take-off had been postponed for an hour, but now the rain had ended. Fog, a worse enemy, was setting in, nevertheless, the flight had been cleared. The big plane lifted off the ground and struggled into the mist. A short time later the apprehensive pilot contacted Kansas City requesting weather reports—suddenly the pilot radioed, "I cannot talk; we are losing altitude—we are going. . . ."

Two farm boys near the little town of Bazaar looked up to see a huge silver plane spinning out of the gray clouds just above their barn. The engine sputtered, followed by a deafening roar. Then parts of what was once the silver wing of the plane lazily floated down from the sky. On April 1, rescuers found Rockne's body on a bleak, wind-swept hill of Bazaar. When they lifted his broken body, his rosary was still held firmly in his hand.

Gus Dorais, his teammate, assistant coach, and lifelong friend, brought his body back in a blue-and-gold draped casket. Every son of Notre Dame, including the Four Horsemen and members of the great 1930 team, was there, weeping. People were stunned. They stared unbelievingly, refusing to accept the news. Messages began to pour in from all over the world. Flowers— acres of them—overflowed the little home, making it necessary to line them in a nearby park.

President Herbert Hoover wired regrets, declaring the tragedy a national loss. Ex-President Coolidge wired, "Rockne was a great man, an inspiring leader, a great teacher. His moral values and right living were the qualities of his great victories." Every important name in the sports field, and sports writers the world over, began a pilgrimage to Notre Dame. Mayor Jimmy Walker came from New York; Rockne's aged mother was there. The King of Norway sent a special delegation of personal representatives. People from every walk of life arrived. An endless stream of visitors moved mournfully past the coffin. Most important, all of his players, almost to the last man, returned to campus. There were representatives of every team he had coached. Weeping, they took up their guard beside the blue-and-gold draped casket. Every store in South Bend was closed, every flag at half mast. A priest sobbing quietly said, "In an age that has stamped itself as the era of 'go getters,' Rockne was a 'go giver.' "—This was not merely a sportsman who had passed away; this was a man.

In 1930 Rockne had made a speech at the Chicago Lions luncheon in which he stated, "I love today, I have seen yester-

afraid of tomorrow." Today is the tomorrow he
erday. Nearly a quarter of a century has passed
he "Great Beyond," but he already has achieved
d to the respect which was always there.

FOUR ATTRIBUTES

The coaching relationship is aimed at maintaining balance in
certain factors affecting you and your players. Those factors are:

1. Success and failure.
2. Pleasure and pain.
3. Security and insecurity.
4. Reward and punishment.

1. Success and Failure

Logic compels us all to agree that life is an interaction of
these four forces. Good mentors strive to establish one at the
exclusion of its counterpart, but never succeed totally. Despite
winning being a fixed objective you would be unrealistic if you
did not prepare to bounce back from failure. All champions come
back. The road to victory is no thruway. It is pocked with ruts
and beset by time-consuming detours which spell failure. While
it is small comfort to the coach and squad that loses, there are,
nevertheless, some advantages which will result. It is when you
are compelled to ride one of the detours that new ideas are born.
Failure compels you to reinspect, then improvise new attacking
formations to compensate for some deficiency. It is the conquest
of failure that makes success dynamic. Success is failure turned
inside out. It must never be inevitable. Nothing succeeds like
success, yet nothing fails like failure. Tell your squad that failure today resulted in the planting of seeds for future victories.
It is similar to the storm that wrecks a harvest yet makes for a
stronger sun for a harvest yet unsown. The "failing-est" man that
ever lived was Thomas Edison, but he bounced back time and
time again to succeed. No one can think of him as a failure
today.

pilot radioed, "I cannot talk; we are losing altitude—we are going. . . ."

Two farm boys near the little town of Bazaar looked up to see a huge silver plane spinning out of the gray clouds just above their barn. The engine sputtered, followed by a deafening roar. Then parts of what was once the silver wing of the plane lazily floated down from the sky. On April 1, rescuers found Rockne's body on a bleak, wind-swept hill of Bazaar. When they lifted his broken body, his rosary was still held firmly in his hand.

Gus Dorais, his teammate, assistant coach, and lifelong friend, brought his body back in a blue-and-gold draped casket. Every son of Notre Dame, including the Four Horsemen and members of the great 1930 team, was there, weeping. People were stunned. They stared unbelievingly, refusing to accept the news. Messages began to pour in from all over the world. Flowers— acres of them—overflowed the little home, making it necessary to line them in a nearby park.

President Herbert Hoover wired regrets, declaring the tragedy a national loss. Ex-President Coolidge wired, "Rockne was a great man, an inspiring leader, a great teacher. His moral values and right living were the qualities of his great victories." Every important name in the sports field, and sports writers the world over, began a pilgrimage to Notre Dame. Mayor Jimmy Walker came from New York; Rockne's aged mother was there. The King of Norway sent a special delegation of personal representatives. People from every walk of life arrived. An endless stream of visitors moved mournfully past the coffin. Most important, all of his players, almost to the last man, returned to campus. There were representatives of every team he had coached. Weeping, they took up their guard beside the blue-and-gold draped casket. Every store in South Bend was closed, every flag at half mast. A priest sobbing quietly said, "In an age that has stamped itself as the era of 'go getters,' Rockne was a 'go giver.' "—This was not merely a sportsman who had passed away; this was a man.

In 1930 Rockne had made a speech at the Chicago Lions luncheon in which he stated, "I love today, I have seen yesterday, and I'm not afraid of tomorrow." Today is the tomorrow he talked about yesterday. Nearly a quarter of a century has passed since he entered the "Great Beyond," but he already has achieved remote love to add to the respect which was always there.

FOUR ATTRIBUTES

The coaching relationship is aimed at maintaining balance in certain factors affecting you and your players. Those factors are:

1. Success and failure.
2. Pleasure and pain.
3. Security and insecurity.
4. Reward and punishment.

1. Success and Failure

Logic compels us all to agree that life is an interaction of these four forces. Good mentors strive to establish one at the exclusion of its counterpart, but never succeed totally. Despite winning being a fixed objective you would be unrealistic if you did not prepare to bounce back from failure. All champions come back. The road to victory is no thruway. It is pocked with ruts and beset by time-consuming detours which spell failure. While it is small comfort to the coach and squad that loses, there are, nevertheless, some advantages which will result. It is when you are compelled to ride one of the detours that new ideas are born. Failure compels you to reinspect, then improvise new attacking formations to compensate for some deficiency. It is the conquest of failure that makes success dynamic. Success is failure turned inside out. It must never be inevitable. Nothing succeeds like success, yet nothing fails like failure. Tell your squad that failure today resulted in the planting of seeds for future victories. It is similar to the storm that wrecks a harvest yet makes for a stronger sun for a harvest yet unsown. The "failing-est" man that ever lived was Thomas Edison, but he bounced back time and time again to succeed. No one can think of him as a failure today.

2. Pleasure and Pain

All cannot be pleasure. Pleasures have value when pain is lurking nearby. Athletics cannot always be fun, especially when learning the fundamentals. Blocking and being blocked, tackling and being tackled is not fun. Running, hitting, fielding, pivoting, shooting are part of a daily routine to bring about proficiency. The road to victory is strewn with pain. Only after being racked with pain do players learn to appreciate fully the fruits of victory.

3. Security and Insecurity

Players must never be made to feel completely secure. It is the threat of insecurity which compels one to put forth his best effort to gain the coveted security. Never do we want to be at either extreme. The extreme right is exactly like the extreme left. You must establish balance. *"Too Much'"* playing time must not give way to *"Not Enough."*

Efficient coaches are constantly aware of the two "P's" during a ball game. They are *"possession* and *position."* These two factors control the times you can play your second and third stringers. If the other team is in possession deep in their own territory, that is the right time and right place to play your substitutes. This will be stimulating to the non-regulars and motivating to your first line group.

4. Reward and Punishment

In utilizing reward and punishment two premises are important:

1. If one does good, make him feel good.
2. If one does not good, make him feel not good.

Any exception to this rule breaks down the learning process.

TWO ADDITIONAL KEYS

There are two more keys which open the doorway leading to good relationship. They are:

1. Not doing what comes naturally.
2. Doing what one dislikes doing.

Not Doing What Comes Naturally

Of equal importance is the knack of never permitting players to do what comes naturally. Only animals and children may engage in activities controlled purely by nature. Only children and animals do what they want, anytime they want.

Doing What One Dislikes Doing

Players must want to do the things they do not like to do. This is the ultimate in coaching. Maturity cannot be achieved until this principle is followed religiously. The drudgery of practice sessions, taking exams, failing, getting up when tired, and later on, working for a livelihood are not activities to which one looks forward with keen anticipation. The milkman who awakens at three in the morning to deliver milk for your babies' breakfast would much rather deliver the previous night and remain in bed until a civilized hour. The doctor who leaves the warmth of his bed to minister to a seriously ill patient; the priest who finds his way into a darkened hospital room, regardless of the weather, to comfort the dying—are doing the things they do not wish to do. Nearly all of us loathe some of our daily tasks, but we have conditioned ourselves to doing what we dislike. Athletics is the fastest medium for the development of this indispensable life trait.

HERD—LEADERSHIP

Smart coaches, as good leaders, make effective use of the herd instinct—the tendency of people to flock together. The word "herd" broken down into individual letters carries the following denotation:

H . . . . Habit.
E . . . . Enthusiasm.
R . . . . Responsibility.
D . . . . Discipline.

These four basic characteristics are vital to team leadership.

1. Habit

Correct habits instill an automatic response to routine situations, thus enabling a coach to apply his talents to the handling of newer and more intricate problems. If it were not for our daily habits, we would still be in the shoebutton era. Habit implies economy of time, thought, and energy. Because coaching involves the development of fundamental habits, the coach and players alike are free to absorb new skills.

2. Enthusiasm

The jet fuel that drives a team is enthusiasm. One spark of real enthusiasm is worth more than ten hours of uninspired drill. It will ignite and fire a team to success. Enthusiasm is infectious.

3. Responsibility

Seeing that everyone accepts the responsibility commensurate with his ability, from the coach down to the last substitute, will result in satisfaction and the successful completion of the job.

4. Discipline

Chapter 5 covers this phase in detail. Every outstanding team is well disciplined. Discipline assures close teamwork and insures good results when the chips are down. Spectators everywhere were impressed with the Army team breaking from the huddle led by their center, racing at flank speed to set up the play, regardless of score. Backs of Oklahoma's outstanding 1956 team covered with opposing humanity literally pushed them off, scrambled to their feet, and raced back to their huddle to obtain a new play. This is the hallmark of a team well disciplined.

CEMENTING YOUR POSITION

with faculty and parents

No man stands as tall as when he stoops to help a boy.

Public Relations in Coaching

Good coaching is likely to be no better than the public understanding of the coach and his techniques. Public relations when
applied to coaching has a special meaning. It is defined as "P"
for performance and "R" for recognition. It is the interpretation
and explanation of what a team is doing. Regardless of how it is
defined, public relations is basically "good relations," among
people in or out of the actual coaching sphere.

A good team is really a collection of good players, but someone must make the public aware of this. Large institutions employ a Director of Public Relations. This procedure often gives
schools the impression that public relations is exclusively associated with a central bureau or office. Nothing is further from
the truth. Public relations cannot be left to the so-called expert.
Actually, it begins the moment the coach is employed and it
never stops. The coach then passes on the major portion of that
responsibility to every player, so their contributions augment his
offering. Together they share a strategic role in interpreting the
team to the school and the people. Good public relations never

permits indifference, misfortune and distrust between players and the public. Because of its importance therefore, creating good public relations is the responsibility of the coach and his charges.

Pride in the Profession

What you are speaks for itself. No one else enjoys the reverence a coach receives in a normal community. It is the nearest thing to the feudal homage of the Dark Ages. Since your conduct will be regarded as a sample of the quality of the profession, never cast undue reflections on the coaching vocation. You come in contact with countless people in a given week; in fact, one game alone exposes you to thousands of pairs of eyes and judgments. Your every move is creating a multitude of impressions. You are a public figure and must live and act accordingly.

In public, never make negative comments about coaches in general, or express a low evaluation of your work. Self-praise may be discounted as biased but self-criticism is always accepted as frankness. Never apologize for the choice of your life work. Pride in the profession is a first requisite to a coach's effectiveness in public relations. To be a good public relationist a coach must thoroughly believe in the truth of the fundamental slogan, "coaches mold our nation's future."

Some Always Rubs Off

When I was in college I received a letter informing me of a very damaging fire which had razed the home of my high school coach. That weekend I went down to console him. He took me to the ruined study where the destruction was complete. Fire had totally consumed his room. This was the very location where many prized moments had been passed, where hundreds of memories were born. In this spot many a touchdown, many a winning game plan had been formulated. All his books were burned —his papers gone.

He pointed it all out and with tears in his eyes he said, "Everything I own is gone—all is destroyed—my books—my valuables—nothing is left." Then I placed my arm around his shoulder in much the same manner as he had done to me when he would speak words of encouragement. I said, "Mr. Wacker, your most valuable possessions were not burned. We, your players, and your player's players, are your most treasured assets. Everything isn't gone—your contributions can never be dissipated."

"As a coach you are always looking over our shoulders. Your influence is constantly felt and is of a lasting quality. You share in our every failure and success, for you helped shape our destinies. Some of you has rubbed off on each and every one of us."

RELATIONSHIP WITH FACULTY MEMBERS

The fact that this relationship is given preferential treatment in the long list of relationships should not surprise you. This division is the most important, for failure to maintain good working relations nullifies your coaching success, regardless of its weight.

The entire faculty must view you as an individual of high integrity. They must view you with deep affection. This profound love and respect must be cultivated: you just do not stumble upon esteem. It results only from painstaking planning of the "give and take."

Three B's

Three "B's" make the heart of this relationship crystal clear. They stand for *"Back" "Boost"* and *"Build." "Back"* your faculty, *"Boost"* your school, and they will *"Build"* your team.

Seek Faculty Cooperation

Do you know the inner working of the teaching family of which you are a part?

Your success depends in part on having a clear picture of the faculty's expectations of you. As a courtesy to you they will return your pledged cooperation. It is therefore imperative that you exercise initiative and tact in cementing this close personal and professional friendship. Your fellow faculty members must know your philosophy of education and athletics in total. If they do not, make them aware of it.

Speak to the principal requesting the privilege of addressing your colleagues. You cannot play mental chess. An efficient principal prepares his faculty meeting agenda at least fifteen days in advance. Get to him before it is fixed and final. Arrange to take not more than ten minutes of the meeting for your message. Do not give lip service, nor have words mask your real feelings. Talk with sincerity; words come naturally if you feel what you say. The objective of your talk is to effect the optimum degree of cooperation between the faculty, players and you.

Inform the faculty that you never look at a player and see just an athlete. Affirm that you view him first and foremost as a pupil. No extra-curricular activity in which a pupil engages can ever replace his important role as a student. Every enterprise in which he is a participant plays a subordinate role to his academic growth. In appraising youngsters you should intend never to separate the athletic field from the classroom.

Advise them that you will refrain from interceding to change a player's standing. You will never foster a false sense of security by having athletes think you can and will tamper with grades. If players refuse to put forth their best efforts in the classroom, you accept as a truism their inclination to loaf during a game.

Emphasize your intent to insist that players view their academic program as most important—that it takes priority. In fact, be adamant in the position that you do not want men on your squad who refuse to work and cooperate with the entire faculty. Only if it is a cooperative and family venture in which the faculty and you march along together will you be happy. Any relationship short of this will create unhappiness. If faculty members can instill responsibility in students while in class, you will realize a subsequent increase in their capacity to play the game. You cannot win games if it is less than a cooperative undertaking. You place yourself in the position that you want to *"serve them"* in return for "being served." One hand washes the other.

Your code should reflect a series of reciprocal expectations and responsibilities. The faculty must feel they are not junior but senior partners in your work.

Minimize the importance of athletics when compared to scholastic achievement, by making all aware of the following conditions. Young people do not obtain positions solely because of athletic proficiency. All the varsity letters, medals, trophies, and membership on mythical "all" teams will not earn their keep; how much they absorbed in class will. Players, and even the sporting public, cannot accurately name last year's all-American team. The American public is prone to forget. Nothing is as old as yesterday's headlines.

Take time to inform the faculty that you are dedicated to a game in which a man's ability is evaluated during the playing of every game. In no other profession is a man's work judged with quicker sarcasm, cynicism, and invective. John Fan loves a winner. No one, not even you, has discovered or invented a substitute for winning. You, of course, are aware of the impossibility of winning them all. It is as impossible as putting toothpaste back in the tube.

Now you make your plea. You implore the faculty to help you do the best possible job under the conditions and philosophy you outlined for them. Tell them you realize your efforts alone will yield only a blemished harvest.

Ask them to give you the cooperation you are willingly offering them. You and they are partners in this work. You must join hands. Your success will now become personally important to them. Welcome them to your practice sessions, and invite them to sit on your bench. Good faculty members will be appreciative, but will never take advantage of your kindness.

Impress them with the necessity for their collaboration so that a rich wholesome experience will accrue to the players.

The faculty should help you not only in the interest of the young men you are coaching but because you are you—a person they know, respect, and like.

When your remarks are completed, you hope their opinions

reflect your gentlemanly qualities. If you have left them with this mental picture of you, your success is in part assured.

CULTIVATE AFFECTION FOR FACULTY MEMBERS

One of the most powerful forces in the building of coaching character is affection. The most common form of its manifestation is gratitude. The exercise of affection makes you tender and loving toward all living persons. The exercise of gratitude results in making them tender and loving toward you. A coach must cultivate this spirit of affection for his fellow faculty members and they will return the same.

We all know what the feeling of gratitude is. We have said "thank you" a million times and have often felt grateful in our hearts for favors and help received. But we are too apt to forget that we have someone to thank for the nice things that creep into our lives. If we would only stop to think, we would soon conclude that all we have done for ourselves is very little indeed, comparable to what has been done for us. An intelligent minister, in describing his elevation to the presidency of the Association of American Clergymen, uttered the following sage statement: "If ever you see a turtle on a tree stump, rest assured someone put it there." If a coach ascends the ladder of success, rest assured a kind and cooperative faculty helped his climb.

I always have liked the story one of my teachers repeated concerning affection and Sir Walter Scott. When Sir Walter was a boy he saw a dog coming toward him and carelessly threw a stone at the stray animal. The stone broke the dog's leg. The poor creature had enough strength and desire left to crawl up to his stoner and pleadingly lick his feet. That wonderful teacher related that Sir Walter later had written that this incident had given him the bitterest remorse of his entire life. He never forgot it. A coach must never cast stones aimlessly.

Abraham Lincoln and Affection

Abraham Lincoln was a poor boy. His early life was full of hardships, but many friends helped him in his struggle with poverty. Among these friends was Jack Armstrong of New Salem, Illinois, whose good-hearted wife offered Lincoln motherly kindness. She made his clothes and fed him and in return, he cared for the baby. Years passed. Lincoln had become a successful lawyer. Jack Armstrong had died. The boy whom Lincoln had rocked was now a grown but wayward young man. He was arrested and charged with murder. Aunt Hannah, as Lincoln used to call her, was grief-stricken. Her tearful appeal to Lincoln to save her boy touched his generous heart. He resolved to discharge his great debt of gratitude, which the intervening years had not erased from his memory, by pledging his services free. Aunt Hannah believed her boy innocent. Lincoln talked with the young man, and was also convinced that he was not guilty. Lincoln worked as hard to free this man as if he was receiving a five thousand dollar fee. He threw his entire soul into the effort to save the life of his client. In the end he succeeded in proving his innocence beyond the shadow of a doubt. His closing plea was a masterpiece of eloquence. He depicted the loneliness and sorrow of the widowed mother, whose husband had once welcomed a strange and penniless boy into his humble home. "That boy now stands before you pleading for the life of his benefactor's son." The verdict was "not guilty." True gratitude never forgets.

Faculty Encouragement

A coach's benefactors are the faculty. He must never alienate their affection. A hostile faculty can break the most successful coach. If your fellow teachers love you, they will supply you with the needed courage to shake off the sting of defeat. They will be your professional mourners. It is their kindness and understanding which gives you the strength and courage to report for practice Monday. They cushion your blow. I have heard this repeated a hundred times: "It's a shame he lost. He deserves a better fate. He is such a fine man. It should not happen to him." In such statements a coach finds true feeling for him. On the other hand, there have been coaches who feel that their success is due only to their own contributions, that players, parents, faculty, give next to nothing. Without their direction no victory could ever be realized. I have heard the following remarks about such indispensable creatures, after they had been defeated: "I hope he loses them all. I hope he doesn't win another damn ball game. He doesn't deserve to be around kids, let alone us. He just doesn't fit. He is an egomaniac."

"A friend in need is a friend indeed." After you have lost a big game, kindness on the part of your peers is a tonic. It is medicine for an ailing heart. Many, many years ago, I read James Whitcomb Riley's poem, *In a Friendly Sort of Way*. The words have returned every time I was befriended by some courteous faculty member:

> When a man ain't got a cent and he's feeling kind of blue,
> And the clouds hang dark and heavy, and won't let the sunshine through,
> It's a great thing, oh, my brethern, for a fellow just to lay
> His hand upon your shoulder in a friendly sort o' way.
>
> It makes a man feel curious, it makes the teardrops start,
> An you sort o' feel a flutter in the region of the heart,
> You can't look up and meet his eyes, you just don't know what to say,
> When a hand is on your shoulder in a friendly sort of way.
> Oh, the world's a curious compound, with its honey and its gall,
> With its cares and bitter crosses, but a good world after all.
> An a good God must have made it—leastwise that is what I say,
> When a hand is on my shoulder in a friendly sort o' way.

Hands of fellow faculty members on your shouders will always give the lift and stimulation that inspires renewed effort.

Conference with Faculty Members

It is an obvious fact that players must pass a fixed proportion of their total academic assignments in order to meet eligibility. During the course of a scholastic year, many athletes come precariously close to the margin. Faculty members whose approval you have won, willingly and without solicitation initiate steps to preserve the players' eligibility. There are times, nevertheless, when a conference with a faculty member appears advisable. This project requires a definite skill. Tact is the key. Someone defined tact as "social lying" and presented this illustration to prove their contention. A young lover holding his best girl's hands, looked into her eyes and said, "Darling, your face would stop a clock." Of course, he was shown the door. On the other hand, another suitor holding her hand looked into her eyes and whispered softly, "Darling, when I look into your eyes, time stands still." Well, the clock was still stopped, but the second young man employed tact and married the girl. So too, diplomacy and tact are important in conferring with a faculty member whose help you need.

It is important as a coach that you realize faculty members desire your approval and your friendship just as you desire theirs. You must therefore never jeopardize this relationship by having a meeting with them construed as a threat to their status. They must be treated with politeness, deference, and dignity. Above all, view them as they really are—equals.

It is suggested that you time your meeting with care. The emotional climate must be propitious. This may require that you "saw wood" waiting for the proper opportunity. The opportunity may present itself over a cup of coffee, at lunch, enjoying a smoke together, or as spectators at a school event. It may be necessary that you visit his classroom or office. Never ask him to come to you, for immediately he may build walls of defensory mechanisms. When the meeting takes place the conversation must allude to a familiar denominator. This sparring for an awaited opening may consume a half hour or more. The key subject is then fitted into the pattern of conversation so adroitly that it appears part of the common plan. Never should your pre-arranged plan manifest its obvious intent. The discussion should not proceed too far along before you convince the faculty member that in your eyes he can do no wrong where the youngster in question is concerned. You must never violate the relationship by being critical of the faculty member. Be careful to avoid any implication of criticism. It is imperative that your colleague be convinced of your general desire to lend your efforts toward improving the youngster's education. Your intent is to work in harmony to establish a program of assistance for the young man, in order that he will pass and be eligible to play.

Your approach is one where you inflate the ego of the faculty member by informing him you are in dire need of help. He alone can help you out of this dilemma. Repeat often that it is up to him—that your contribution will be only a guarantee to carry out the plan he proposes. The conference should consist of unbalanced conversation. He talks and you listen. Only when you feel there is a deviation from your prearranged plan do you inject a pivotal comment to restore the thread of your original objective.

The next phase of the conference deals with the implementation of its results. Here there must be no violation of some basic principles, the most basic being that the faculty member will handle the situation alone from here in. The coach's only duty is to remind the player in question to see his teacher. Never should the coach assume responsibility for carrying out the plan.

Saved—One Tackle

Perhaps an actual incident occurring during my tenure at La Salle High School will explain this technique.

In 1938 I had a tackle named Gus Cifelli. He had enrolled at La Salle with the intent of playing football. All other considerations were secondary, including the academic program. He studied, of course, because it was an obstacle to be conquered in order to play.

During the second semester of his junior year,, he failed a course and decided to leave school. My problem was to keep him in school regardless of football participation. I did want him to continue in athletics, but primarily I wished him to succeed in his scholastic program.

I decided to enlist the aid of the teacher, for an entire future life was at stake. Planning to meet the teacher was an easy task. I deliberately, by accident, placed myself outside his office just about the time he stepped out for lunch. I asked him to join me. Over a sandwich and a cup of coffee we discussed many things, all foreign to football.

The proper emotional climate had been established. I then inquired outright whether he would help me with a personal problem. "Of course," he replied. I then proceeded to describe how much school was doing for Gus Cifelli, how his life had changed since coming to high school, how much he liked to play football. I pointed out that someday he would grow academically as well as athletically. If he quit school, my objective for his all-around development would never be realized. I made it clear that we could reach Cifelli through what he liked best—football. That was our opening—the gateway to his entire life, for football made his existence meaningful. As a special favor to me and the boy, would the teacher be willing to cooperate to save the future of this boy by giving him special tutoring after school and any other time it could be arranged? With care I pointed out that I did not object to Cifelli not practicing in order to improve his grades. I impressed him with the importance of this task. A life was at stake. The fact that I, as coach, would release him from practice was sufficient evidence of my personal interest in this young man.

Notice with care how important I made the English teacher feel. He alone controlled the turning point, and the entire future of the boy's life. The faculty member accepted the challenge. He promised to help.

I then proceeded to have a private conference with Cifelli, and convinced him that to miss a week's practice in place of losing out entirely was good logic. Cifelli was impressed with the profundity of my desire to help, along with the sincerity of the English teacher.

Vindication for this undertaking was evidenced in Gus Cifelli's graduation from Notre Dame in 1945 with a philosophy major—then four years with the champion Detroit Lions football team. Today he is employed by the Ford Motor Company in the capacity of Chief of Personnel.

The Uncooperative Faculty Member

Although teaching has developed into a profession, there are still some teachers who employ unprofessional tactics, and you will make their acquaintance.

There are two kinds of people. People who do things and people to whom things are done. A coach must be both. In this instance, disillusioned teachers will do things to you. They suffer from such severe cases of teacher paranoia that seeking their cooperation is futile. These disgruntled faculty members will criticize you and the school in general. Pity their plight, allow them to relive their failures, but make no attempt to approach them. Take your licking, if necessary. Be polite to them and avoid unnecessary contacts with them so their destructive attitude does not rub off on you.

The basic tenet of this section is worthy of repetition. The only reason you approach a colleague at all is not solely to have the pupil play, but to serve him by insuring his scholastic growth. What accrues to you as a coach is merely a byproduct of this planned action.

Game Exploitation

Occasions will arise when faculty members will look with envy and bitterness upon the fanfare accorded to athletics as contrasted to the apathy shown for their activity. Your lip service on cooperation to these people is often insufficient. Tangible evidence is sometimes needed. You may meet this problem area by extending the interest in your sport to their phases of the school program. This type of cooperation with faculty members who are supervising other activities will improve the efficiency of your public relations. The following techniques are suggested.

At games, the loud speaker equipment could be used by a teacher to tell about other school achievements, especially those that are timely. Typical "fillers" in the program may include facts about school growth, the inadequate facilities that the band conquered to obtain its present proficiency, and the academic rating of the school by the recent evaluation.

Another teacher, in charge of the public address system at football games, may use "quiet" and "time out" moments to insert statements about other worthwhile student activities.

This would also be an appropriate time to emphasize community events as well as the after-the-game dance.

THE COACH AND THE PARENT

The lines "The hand that rocks the cradle is the hand that rules the world" were written nearly a century ago, but time has not dimmed their veracity. The relationship of the coach and parent is a most vital one.

At the turn of the century, young men deemed it a privilege to participate in athletics. In fact, sports were one of the few outlets for young people aspiring to early fame. However, within the last twenty years, new horizons have appeared which have necessitated drastic changes.

Attitudes toward athletic participation vary today, and you are compelled to compete for the boy's interest and time. Television, theatres, clubs, and the desire to work and buy a car take precedence over athletic competition in the eyes of a young man. Good coaches understand early the need to nullify the strong effect of these outside forces.

Reaching the parent could be the turning point. Coaches who concentrate solely on winning the admiration and affection of their players are operating in a kind of vacuum.

Parents Are Not Enemies

Parents are not your natural enemies, as some coaches are wont to believe. Parents will support you as long as they believe your work is in the interest of their children, and not at the expense of their children. If difficulties do arise, it is because a parent's interest is inevitably spotlighted on his own child while your concern is for *all* the team members.

Regardless of the few complaints which normally arise, your

relationship with the parent must, of necessity, be professional, close, and personal. Above all, pains must be taken to make it pleasant and helpful without losing your individuality.

You must understand at the start that parents are not trained as coaches. They judge everything through eyes which see only their youngsters. It should be that way, and you would not have it otherwise. If you can integrate this parental interest by helping them interpret the game your way, you will never have to conform to their selfish desires. You will never need to sacrifice your basic convictions about successful coaching in the mere interest of pleasing some parent.

Learn to disagree with parents agreeably. If you observe others who tend to antagonize a parent you will find that generally it is the way in which people disagree that becomes obnoxious. You can express different views without wavering and without offending any but the most sensitive.

Years ago, West Chester was playing a heavier Youngstown University team. By means of the swivel-hipped running of our 130 lb. Dickie Wolf, we moved to the three-yard line. At this point Youngstown substituted its heaviest linemen. Two thrusts by the slightly built Wolf resulted in no gain. Head Coach Killinger substituted a bigger but slower back, and we scored. Following the game, Mr. Wolf asked why his son was not permitted to stay in the game and score. I explained carefully the need to meet weight with weight—that two tries by Dick had failed to produce a touchdown. I emphasized that the touchdown was made possible only through the efforts of his son. Did he wish his son to be a hero or did he prefer that West Chester insure a score? Which objective would he choose?

PERSONAL APPEARANCE TOURS

Hollywood stars find that appearing in person stimulates public interest in their screen productions. You must steal a page from their book.

Long before the season gets under way, call a meeting of aspiring candidates. Consult with your principal and request permission to visit the home of each. Inquire about the feasibility of sending letters to the parents, informing them of your desire to visit their homes, in view of the new relationship which will result from their boy's expressed desire to participate in your sport.

It is suggested that the letter be personalized. A form letter has little impact on the recipient. Above all, care should be taken that the composition of the letter does not convey the impression of prying.

The salutation should be: "Dear Mr. and Mrs. Smith." The letter should be signed by both the principal and the coach, and in the left hand corner of the envelope, write the word "Personal." My experiences have led me to believe that such a marking on an envelope has much more meaning to a parent. It immediately arouses a feeling of closeness for it conveys a kinship that you and the parent share alone. A sample letter follows:

> Dear Mr. & Mrs. Smith,
>
> Your boy, Joseph, has made the coaching staff very happy by his expressed desire of being a candidate to represent Roosevelt High School on the gridiron this season.
>
> It is the opinion and the philosophy of the coaches that they can better serve and aid your son if they know something more about him and his family.
>
> With that thought in mind, may we have the privilege of visiting with you for a few moments at a time convenient to you?
>
> On the enclosed card will you please check the day and time when a member of our coaching staff may visit with you.
>
> Thank you very much for your cooperation, which will result in a better understanding of everyone concerned.
>
> Yours truly,
>
> John Fitz,
> Coach

John Doe
Principal

The Visit

The actual visit procedure will vary in order to adapt to prevailing conditions. In some homes you will find it difficult to make conversation. In others you will be delegated to the role of a listener. A prudent coach will find something in every home to praise or admire. Mention of some admirable quality of the youngster should also be a part of every coach–parent conference.

Regardless of the situation, you must leave parents with the impression that you are most happy over the prospect of having their boy participate. Promise them that mutual benefits will accrue. Leave them with a feeling that they may call on you anytime in the interest of their boy. Your visit should be limited to a maximum of 15 minutes.

A well-trained coach can enter the front door, walk slowly through a home toward the back door, and make observations concerning a youngster's background. The way parents greet you, their cordiality and general appearance, the physical condition of the home, and the type of reading material in evidence are little keys to a better understanding.

Armed with this new insight about each player you now can begin to individualize your coaching.

Familiarity Breeds Contentment

Surely you have heard it stated "contempt" in lieu of contentment. If parents are happy, their youngsters will reflect their attitude. One method of keeping parents—especially father— happy, is through the following contrivance.

Invite a few fathers to accompany the team in the school bus. By calling upon different ones for each game, you avoid the appearance of favoritism. It is essential that no parent be permitted within the inner sanctum of your dressing room. Have them help with some chore which is isolated from the team's pre-game preparations, such as holding the 10 yard marker, and checking the bench for equipment arrangements.

The Coach—A Man of Letters

There are two additional instances when you will want to write personal letters to the parent. They occur while the season is in progress and after its completion. Postal praise is a strong asset for you to utilize.

Every candidate will achieve some worth-while objective sometime during the season, otherwise you have not coached. Perhaps his tremendous effort has won a game. Perhaps his practicing every day with the Jay-Vees to sharpen the varsity will be a contribution worthy of note.

Letters expressing glowing praise of their youngsters should be sent to the parents at least once during a season.

Here is an example of a letter expressing a mid-season situation.

> Dear Mr. and Mrs. Smith,
>
> Certainly you saw our Varsity play Lincoln High School last week. Most spectators, however, do not realize the many, many factors which help produce a sharp team. There are substitute and Jay-Vee players who never play at game time, but whose constributions are a major factor in winning. Without the unselfish efforts of each of these young men, our school could never field a team.
>
> Your son, as a member of the Jay-Vee squad, has had a hand in every victory. It his effort, together with others, in daily practice which results in the proficiency of the Varsity.
>
> This loyalty without public acclaim, day in and day out, can result only because you fine parents have made him the fine boy that he is.
>
> The coaching staff wants to convey their deepest appreciation for your cooperation.
>
> Yours truly,
>
> John Fitz,
> Coach

Paving the Way

At the end of the season, regardless of the record, letters must be sent home thanking parents for their cooperation. This serves a twofold purpose, for in addition to thanking them, you pave the way to renewed cooperation for next year's team. An example follows.

To Thank You

Dear Mr. & Mrs. Smith,

Roosevelt High School has just completed another successful football season. The coaching staff realizes only too well the many people whose cooperation and loyalty made this possible.

You, as parents, must be singled out for your aid during the past season. All players leave the jurisdiction and eyes of the coach immediately upon leaving the practice field, and a great many destructive forces tug at them. An extension of the coaches' vigilance is necessary. That you fine people have taken up that needed supervision has been evidence by Johnny's contribution.

The staff wishes to apologize for your many late dinners, for family disruptions, for concern over bruises his play inflicted. Only altruistic people would put up with these upsetting conditions.

Believe me, we are all grateful for your understanding.

May God bless you and keep you and your family well.

Yours truly,

John Fitz,
Coach

The Special Contact

There are marked occasions when a special communique must be sent to the parents. It would be prudent for you to place the names of every candidate on your calendar to mark their birthdays—then send them a card at their homes. This gesture is most heartwarming, and gives you that extra trump to strengthen your hand in the absolute control of the boy.

Christmas is another time of the year when cards are sent to the players and parents.

This interest must not stop with the completion of the season. If a player becomes ill during the year, visit him at home or at the hospital. Show a solicitous attitude for his welfare by frequent calls.

A few minutes or even an hour invested in this fashion will pay huge dividends during the season.

chapter three

THE THREE MUSTS IN RELATIONSHIPS

Assistants——Community——Press

No one can cheat you out of ultimate success but yourself
—SCHILLER

Robert Hutchins, when President of the University of Chicago, summed up his success in the following sentence, "I have been fortunate in my undertakings by surrounding myself with assistants who know more than I do."

Dr. Hutchins could have easily been Coach Hutchins explaining the need for good assistants. Behind every head coach one will find a select group termed "assistants," who put the coaching machinery in motion. In modern athletics, no head coach can possibly spread himself thin enough to cover every detail. He must depend on the ability of his aides.

Importance of Good Assistants to Team Success

Oftentimes the uninformed public thinks of an assistant as someone whose knowledge is inferior to that of the head coach. This premise does not always follow. Without the assistant who is a specialist, head coaches would soon be out of business. Their shingles would come down overnight. Usually the head coach plans the strategy, but its implementation rests squarely upon the shoulders of an assistant.

Wilkinson of Oklahoma is one of the finest coaches in our country. His record is ample evidence, but without his outstanding assistants, especially line coach Gomer Jones, it is conceivable he might soon be an also ran. Of course, being a head coach requires the uncanny ability of hiring competent assistants. A coach is the head man because he can issue orders that can be carried out. Assistants must carry them out and execute his wishes.

Regardless of the competency of your aides, there are some definite problem areas. Unless you are all trained at the same institution, some adjustments are mandatory. To be an assistant coach requires absolute loyalty even in the face of not believing in the program. Where loyalty comes with difficulty, you should insist on a parting of the ways.

Players always suffer, as well as team efficiency, when the coaching family is disrupted. The objective of a disloyal coach is to hurt his fellow workers instead of concentrating upon the development of player skills. Just as a youngster suffers in a discordant home, so too, players lose out when coaches fail to work as a harmonious team.

All clashes between coaching personalities divide the loyalty of the team.

Meeting Assistants for the First Time

First things must be done first. In this instance an explanation of your system of play is a must. Every coach must be thoroughly familiar with your basic offensive and defensive patterns. Tell them they are free to make suggestions; merely insist they can defend the suggested alterations. A portion of this explanation of your basic system of play should include sound reasons for its employment. You must convince your aides of the soundness of your system—that it fits the material at hand. Once this phase has been established then you discuss your practice organization. You inquire about the drills they have used successfully and suggest some of your own.

In some instances it will be necessary to coach the assistants, so they in turn will be ready to coach the players. This process may consume a month's time with daily secret meetings and practices. It is imperative that this procedure be withheld from the players.

In 1946 I assumed my coaching duties at West Chester State Teachers College knowing very little about the "T" formation and its intricacies. Previous to this assignment I had coached the "Notre Dame Formation." Head Coach Glenn Killinger took me aside every day for a month to explain the five "T" blocking techniques, plus the system of communicating them. During these meetings he convinced me that it was no longer necessary for linemen to memorize a specific assignment for each play. Numbering the offensive team instead of the defense made for consistency in the offensive pattern. The linemen had only to master which of the five blocking patterns were to be employed to open the hole at the point of attack. Play number *six—sixteen—one hundred and six—a million and six*—all referred to the *six hole*. The system was unbelievably simple.

When Mr. Killinger questioned me on defenses, he soon learned that I lacked his broad vision concerning collegiate defenses. He explained his desire to have his defensive linemen one yard back of the line of scrimmage. To surrender such yardage and compel the rush to initiate from such a deep position failed to impress me. His answers to a few questions convinced me of the validity of his alignment.

Before the end of the month I knew exactly what he wished me to teach. We had reached a meeting of the minds. I was so convinced that convincing the players was a simple matter.

Without this preliminary explanation I probably would have taught fundamentals foreign to the play pattern. Youngsters would not have received the necessary training to fit his system of play; in fact, confusion and a lack of discipline would have resulted.

If this plan fails to produce the type of assistants you want, then begin to look for some who are, with the intent of eventually convincing the administration of the need for hiring these select men.

God gave food to every bird but he didn't exactly place it in their nests. It may be necessary for you to look for able assistants.

The Regular Sunday Meeting with Assistants

One of the most successful routines occurs when you, as head coach, invite your assistants to your home on the Sunday evening preceding the following week's game. If they are married, invite their wives. The wives chat while you and your helpers retreat to some secluded area to formulate plans.

At this meeting you meticulously analyze the scouting report. New plays are designed and you agree upon a defense. This is followed by a session from which general game strategy emerges. You and your assistants will make suggestions and then attack them. This process tests the validity of the new offerings. I have been in some coaching meetings which would put a labor union gathering to shame.

As a head coach you do not want spineless "yes-men." If your aides are "yes-men," the chances are they merely want to win your approval. This practice may flatter you for a brief time, but in the long run you will lose respect for them. On the other hand, if they are "no-men," always finding fault with your procedures, eventually you will lose confidence in them. "Yes-men" and "no-men" are equally disliked and mistrusted. You need front line assistants with open minds; men who are capable of sizing up a situation and who help provide a workable solution. Their "yes" or "no" should signify an honest opinion and be coupled with intelligent suggestions. Any assistant who violates this principle must go. You cannot be successful with vacillating aides.

As the meeting progresses, all differences of opinion should be ironed out to keep the meeting from going off on a tangent. If you fail to reach a settlement on controversial matters, you will waste valuable practice hours.

In dealing with such discussions you, as head coach, must avoid any display of temper which will discourage future contributions by your help. However, when you do assign a responsibility to an assistant, you must insist that it be carried out. If you can have him accomplish it without intricate supervision on your part, then you have a real aide.

By the time the evening is terminated, everyone is happy that a constructive winning plan has been born. It is of the utmost importance that every assistant believes implicitly in the final plans. Under no conditions will you tolerate second guessing in your immediate coaching family.

Making Practice Plans with Your Assistants

The Sunday meeting will reveal practice plans for the ensuing week. It is wise for you to designate certain areas on the practice field where special groups will drill. It would be prudent for you actually to go out on the field with your assistants and single out these locations.

The specific practice plan should provide for the time element. It must include the amount of time to be allotted to each phase of the game. You must guard against this aspect of coaching becoming trial and error. Specific systems and procedures for their realization must be definitely established. There must be a time and place for everything, and everything in its place at the right time. A portion of a typical practice chart worked out with your assistants should unfold as follows:

WEEK OF SEPT. 3-8TH (*Central High Game*)

Monday   MONDAY

BACKS
- 3-3:45 . . . . Pass defense. Central offense.
- 3:45-4 . . . . Blocking practice.
- 4-4:20 . . . . Run new plays.
- 4:20 on . . . . Group work.

LINE
- 3-3:30 . . . . Shoulder and cross blocks.
- 3:30-4 . . . . Defensive end drill.
- 4-4:20 . . . . Run new plays.
- 4:20 on . . . . Group work.

GROUP	4:20-4:30	Talk on merit of last week's play —need for this approaching game.
	4:30-5:15	Dummy scrimmage with emphasis on new plays.
	5:15-5:30	Sprints.

Tuesday   TUESDAY

BACKS	3-3:15	Pass defense and running defense.
	3:15-3:30	New plays.
	3:30	Group work.
LINE	3-3:15	Tackling drills.
	3:15-3:30	Blocking drills.
	3:30	Group work.
GROUP	3:30-4:45	Scrimmage against Central's defense and offensive pattern.
	4:45-5:15	Kicking scrimmage.
	5:15	All in.

This chart hung on the coaches' bulletin board enables each one to know exactly what the other is doing. Interference with your assistants is then held to a minimum. It is most discouraging to your aides to begin a drill and then have you interrupt it. Anything short of this organizational pattern will lead to confusion and chaos.

Making Demands on Assistants Through an Indirect Approach

As head coach, insist that every assistant plunge into his work with the same zeal and enthusiasm you do. As their leader, give them their just due. Tell the student body, press, and players that team success is not due to your contributions but to the outstanding ability of your assistants. Praise them to the skies.

There is, however, one very important element to carry out when dealing with assistants. You work, plan, eat, shower, and dress together but there is always a little of you which they must never know and master. Never have them feel a hundred per cent secure. This is a must, for there will come a time when you turn on the heat, not on your assistants directly, but through the team. You, of course, by subtle inference include the coaches. For instance, never allude to the end coach by name, but say emphatically at a meeting that you are dissatisfied with the work of the ends. Address your remarks directly to the ends, but make sure that the end coach is within earshot of your voice.

It may be wise to say to the ends that, beginning tomorrow, you want them to practice blocking until they can move a tackle a full yard. Mr. Jones (end coach) will work with them. If Mr. Jones' blood is red, and it is, he will squirm uncomfortably. He will chafe at the bit, but you can bet that the ends will get a going over tomorrow—and you obtain results. It is unnecessary to talk to your end coach directly. In order to add more pressure walk over and observe the end coach working with his men during the next practice session.

Private Conferences with Assistants

There will be times when this subtle approach will fail, and a private conference will be in order, in which you will offer constructive criticism. This is always done on an impersonal basis. Damn the work, but not the person. Focus your attention more on the error than the man who is responsible. If, on the other hand, the end coach has achieved your desired wishes—praise him publicly. Tell the ends, within earshot of their end coach, how happy you are with their improvement.

No coach can realize success by taking all the pressure off of his assistants. You love them but you apply the needle at times in order to insure results.

Frank Leahy and His Assistants

In 1951, I was privileged to spend a week observing Frank Leahy direct his spring practice at Notre Dame. He had a unique relationship with his assistant coaches. Every one of his assistants could have been a head coach in his own right, yet they chose to remain with him. (Proof of the last statement is in the fact that after Leahy's retirement from coaching they accepted head coaching responsibilities.) Of course, Leahy always insisted that his aides be well paid. He praised them publicly, but he also blistered them with scathing remarks.

I recall vividly Leon Hart and Jim Martin, two men who later blossomed into All-American stature, missing practice one day. Frank Leahy from atop his wooden throne situated in the middle of the field barked at the end coach, demanding the whereabouts of the two men. The end coach replied he did not know. "See that they get here tomorrow," ordered Leahy. A curt "Yes, sir" was the assistant's reply. The next day they were there and every practice day thereafter. The end coach was a personal friend of mine, and I said to him, "Johnny, next year you will be saluting that man."

Right then and there I learned clearly why Frank Leahy's teams were among the best in the nation, year in and year out. It was his uncanny ability to drive his coaches so their efforts equalled that of the players.

The Technique of Reprimanding an Assistant

There are very few times when this is necessary, but when the need does arise you should know the technique to utilize.

Repeated trivial offenses and more serious derelictions by an assistant call for some sort of private reprimand. It can range from a mild rebuke to a thorough bawling out. Its purpose is to make your assistant agree that he has made a mistake and to resolve to make corrections. It is important to remember that any coaching error always results in damage to the players personally and to the team in general.

Once you are sure of your facts, don't beat around the bush. Arrange a private session with your aide. Get to the point quickly. Keep calm and collected, but remain firm. Avoid becoming angry or starting an argument.

Carry the reprimand as far as necessary, but be sure you are improving morale, not destroying it. A thin skinned person often gets as much from a mild reproof as a hard character does from an old-fashioned dressing down. Suit the severity of the reprimand to the seriousness of the offense. Do not threaten. Chances are that the high school assistant knows you can only recommend a termination of his coaching duties.

A good coach can reprimand in such a manner that the assistant understands exactly where he has transgressed. You must leave him with the feeling that the reprimand was deserved. The subordinate must know too, that unless the error is repeated, nothing more will ever be said about it.

It is relatively easy to bawl out an aide, but your real job is to rebuild and make him more valuable. To accomplish this, you, as head coach, must guide him in the formation of corrective actions.

After your talk has been completed, make sure you are friendly and hold no grudge. By all means, do not let your assistant go away angry. Nagging is out. It would make you as unpopular as a nagging mother-in-law. It is an admission that you have failed in your reprimand.

Perhaps two personal experiences will illustrated this technique.

The "Substitute Happy" Assistant's Blunder

The first took place in 1940 when I was still in high school coaching. My backfield coach was so enthusiastic and concerned with winning that often he substituted without regard for the game clock.

I must say that all assistants should be entrusted with making the substitutions in their specialties. This practice compels players in question to respect the assistant on an equal footing with the head coach. The end coach substitutes the ends; the center coach the center; and so on.

This young coach substituted illegally, causing the team to suffer a five yard penalty at least once a game. Invariably we won and I merely cautioned him to be more careful in substituting. As the season progressed it became increasingly evident that our team was in title contention. During the fourth quarter of our seventh game with the score 0-0 and our team in possession four yards from a possible score, I was appalled to see a substitute enter the game. My backfield assistant had substituted another fullback while the clock was still running. The officials stepped off five yards. Our team ran four plays and didn't score. The ball was resting on the two yard line where our opponents took over, and the game ended in a scoreless deadlock.

While the men were dressing, I informed my assistant that he had an appointment with me at 8:15 Monday morning. When he entered my office I met and greeted him as I would under any other circumstance. I then proceeded to inform him that he was too good and too intelligent a coach to be guilty of such elementary errors in substituting. I inquired whether or not he desired this year's team to reminisce twenty years later and realize that an imprudent substitution caused them to lose the title. "Our kids work too hard—they battle like hell for every yard—and then you take some away from them. I won't stand for it. I don't want these kids hurt again. Here is a listing of the occasions when the game clock is stopped. Only at these stipulated times may you substitute. You are too valuable to this ball club for me to be compelled to restrict you to the observation phone instead of the bench. Please be careful. We must not let the kids down." With that I excused myself for another appointment.

Be Realistic in Disciplining Players

The second incident took place early in my college coaching career.

One of my defensive tackles was not penetrating deeply enough, so I pulled him out. When he reached the sideline, I placed my arm around him and began an explanation of his deficiency. He turned to me in wrath, blaming the end for the gains and absolving himself. I walked away to avoid a scene.

That young man did not play any more that game. I also refused to play him during the next game. I had taken his outburst as a personal affront. I will not stand for anything except "yes sir" and "no sir," during a game. I did notice, however, that keeping this player out of the next game hurt our team, for it compelled a man to play sixty minutes. In modern day football that is asking too much. The efficiency of our team was considerably impaired because of the fatigue element. I noticed it but was adamant in not playing the recalcitrant tackle.

The next day our head coach, Glenn Killinger, called me in for a personal conference. He convinced me that refusing to play the man in question at the time of his outburst was sufficient punishment. To go on holding a personal grudge was equivalent to placing team success second to my personal prestige. "You are too big to do that. The success of this team is most important. Talk to the boy. He is a sophomore and needs the experience for next year." In a tone of command he said, "Jim, I want that man to play." He did.

Train Your Assistant to Take Your Job

A good head coach passes on his training and "know how" to his understudy, in order that he may take his place. It is loyal, not disloyal, for your assistants to observe and train themselves to take your job when you are ready for promotion or retirement.

If a good relationship exists, you will be the first to recommend your assistant for the headship. It is heart warming for you to know that your coaching is respected to the point where one of your trainees is chosen as your successor.

A Special Kind of Help

An important side light to this relationship must be discussed here. Every head coach discovers certain phases of the game in which he has a decided weakness. It is wise to hire assistants who can compensate for this lack by relieving you of that facet of coaching.

It is a subtle move made with the knowledge of both men, yet neither states it in words. Sometimes a good assistant becomes aware of the head man's weakness and says nothing about it. The subordinate cleverly relieves the head coach of that duty and takes it upon himself because he is better suited.

It is wise to repeat that the main objective of an assistant coach is to blend all his efforts to make the head coach more successful.

Reflected Glory

Seize every possible opportunity to co-star your assistants. If you are giving information to the press or radio, include the contributions of your aides. Whenever pictures are taken for the local paper, school magazine, or yearbook, go out of your way to include photos of your helpers.

Spotlighting Your Assistants

At school rallies, have your assistants take turns speaking. Your role should be restricted to an introduction or total absence from the platform. In evaluating Ed Sullivan, a television critic wrote, "the reason why TV stars and viewers like Ed Sullivan, as a master of ceremonies, is that he never steals an act. He introduces the star and unobtrusively fades away." As a head coach, you should develop that faculty.

It is annoying to find head coaches who do very little of the actual coaching suddenly coming to life to occupy the spotlight.

Focusing attention on your assistants will result in renewed and inexhaustible efforts on their part. A pat on the back at the right time will pay dividends. All men are praise-conscious regardless of the position they enjoy. Big men do big things. Be big.

Assistants as Balance Wheels

Deftness in utilizing assistants as balance wheels when handling a special player-coach problem is psychologically important. Perhaps an example will best illustrate this skill.

Years ago, I had an excellent tackle, Jones, who had two years of playing experience behind him. He was the outstanding lineman in our league. Prior to the opening of the season we trained at Ocean City, N. J.

It was our custom to free the players in the evening to walk the boards, with a 10 o'clock curfew. That meant in bed with lights out at 10—not merely in their rooms.

On the fourth night, bed check revealed the absence of our star tackle. I immediately called a conference with my line coach.

At eleven thirty the young man returned. I asked for an explanation. The moment he uttered two words I snapped, "That's enough!" I pulled out my wallet and handed him $5.00 for fare home on the first train in the morning. He was crushed. I walked away with the fear of a bootlegger who has learned he has just sold a revenue agent his still. His repeated attempts to talk with me in my room met a stern refusal. The player was ordered to depart in the morning.

My assistant soon visited the boy, listened to his story and promised to intercede for him, but made no commitment. He also instructed the young lineman not to leave until he had heard from him.

At 9 o'clock the next morning my aide informed the boy that, despite repeated pleadings, my position was unmoved. The youngster practically wept, and begged for another chance. The assistant said, "I'll talk to the Coach again, but you must understand that he does not tolerate breaking training rules."

At 10:30, the line coach returned to inform the tackle that he could remain but had to produce, otherwise the aide would be embarrassed.

In this episode, there was not one instant when the head coach and assistant were not working in harmony as parties to the collusion. Had this young man left the squad as ordered I would have cut my throat. He was bread and butter.

I did help save face in the eyes of the squad for rescinding the order by stating to the tackle so everyone could hear, "Jones, you have your line coach to thank for your being here. I hope he did the right thing." This makes you the villain and your assistant becomes a hero. Your position as head coach helps balance out his hatred for you. Remember his efficiency takes precedence over your popularity.

I recall instances in my present position when our head coach was down on a player and repeatedly bawled him out. Being a spectator to these incidents, I undertook steps to nullify the hurt in order not to lose a good ball player. Immediately I sought the boy after practice or visited with him in his room. My intent was never to side with the young man. If the head coach thought he was loafing, then he was. My intent was to convince the boy that I was going to help him convince the boss man that he was hustling again.

Listen—Look—Stop

Misunderstandings must be considered as danger signals comparable to the sign at a railroad crossing which cautions one to "Stop, Look, Listen." The only difference is that the assistant rearranges the sign to read "Listen, Look, Stop."

The assistant *"listens"* to the player patiently and open-mindedly, and allows him to talk the problem out. He then *"looks"* at the problem objectively, weighing all the facts. This is followed by *"stopping"* the causes behind the grievance, and presenting facts to show the young man he is wrong. You accomplish this by presenting the head coach's viewpoint. The conference should terminate with the young man more determined than ever to make up for his omission.

I am not abashed to write that I have successfully convinced young men to apologize to the head coach even when the player was absolutely right and the man in charge was wrong. The young players in question to this very day do not know they were right.

As head coach, you must discuss this sleight of hand with your assistants. If you can develop them into successful balance wheels, your coaching vehicle will never need towing.

RELATIONSHIP WITH THE COMMUNITY

It takes full time living with a community and its people for a coach to understand what goes on above and beneath the surface.

Full time teaching and coaching duties will make this quite a chore but some *"musts"* present themselves. You must identify yourself with various community agencies. Joining service clubs, veterans' organizations, and affiliating with your church denomination will somewhat ease these problems. As all parents and players share in local activities, they will be pleased to see their coach participating in community enterprises. It is unnecessary to say that the coach's life will be enriched, too.

Do Not Attempt Changes

Slowly but surely, you begin a program of collecting and analyzing factual information. The program must cover all aspects of people and their culture as it appears in a geographical area. The survey should concentrate on customs, sport traditions, player characteristics, group leaders, social tensions, and the history of past community athletic efforts. Once these are known only an unwise or wealthy coach will run counter to established policies and evoke criticism.

The customs and mores of your community should be respected. Remember not only is the community tolerant of you, but you too are expected to be understanding of its history.

These customs were not developed overnight and no newcomer is apt to change them quickly.

Don't Be a Suitcase Coach

The coach should enter into some community activities to a reasonable degree, especially those concerned with athletics. Too frequent absences from the community over the weekend are regarded unfavorably. Communities look very critically upon the suitcase coach who never truly identifies himself with the community in which he coaches.

A discussion of the most important community agencies with which a coach should be affiliated follows:

The Church

You and your family should be active members of your local church. Perhaps your wife can volunteer her services as a teacher in the Sunday School, or as an advisor to some "young people's group." Certainly she should become a member of the "Ladies Aid Society." In so doing, your wife will cement and enhance your role as a constructive member of the community. Your children should also be active participants in all appropriate church functions.

You and your family should attend church services with regularity. This symbolic joining of hands with some of your players in an adoration of God strengthens your overall position.

Service Clubs

Service clubs can be a potent factor in your desire to build an effective community relationship. It would be a grave error to neglect the many opportunities presented through these groups.

Service clubs are in constant search of speakers engaged in community enterprises. You will endear yourself to every program chairman by offering your services as a seasonal speaker for one of their meetings. The successful fulfillment of this activity will result in a two-fold reward. First, community interest in the team is stimulated and maintained. Secondly, you, as its coach, are kept in the public eye.

Do not be carried away with enthusiasm by promising your listeners more than you can deliver. Good coaches are always reserved in evaluating their ball clubs. You constantly moan about material and chances of winning. Regardless of how fine your material is you never have enough. Later if you win, it is a pleasant surprise. If you lose, your promises can never return to haunt you. You didn't make any. Be cautious in your critical analysis of anyone or anything. Only coaches with great winning records behind them are permitted to evaluate athletics.

Some time ago, Bobby Bragan, at the time manager of the Pittsburgh Pirates, was relieved of his duties. His discharge was caused primarily by his willingness to speak his mind. His observations were usually correct but he lacked the years of managerial service needed to offer criticism. Stengel and Durocher could have been quoted and no injury to their personal prestige would have resulted.

I want to sum up this aspect of coach-assistant relationship by quoting former Secretary of Defense Wilson. He is reported to have said at a Congressional hearing, "As the mamma whale said to her calf, it is only when you are blowing that you are liable to be harpooned." Beware that your remarks do not make you a target for a harpoon.

Patronizing Local Sporting Merchants

A special community relationship is one concerned with the purchasing of equipment. Salesmen intent on selling their wares are constantly beating a path to your dressing room. As an impartial coach, you will not want to offend anyone, yet you cannot purchase from all. There are certain guide posts which can be of service to you in solving this dilemma.

First, you should buy equipment manufactured by front line, well-established companies. It may cost more but it will last longer. Saving money on equipment is false economy. It robs the youngster of adequate protection and robs the spectator, who is viewing a poorly equipped team. Saving three hundred dollars a year, and then having a key back injured is poor business. It reminds me of the Indian whose blanket wasn't long enough to cover his neck. He solved his problem by cutting off some of the bottom and sewing it on to the top. It will pay you to buy the best.

Your problem is at this point only partially solved, for nearly all sporting goods stores in the community handle front-line products. It is necessary to make a choice. Pick up the phone and call nearby schools and colleges. Inquire about the calibre of service these stores render. By "service" I mean emergency situations, when you need a new pair of shoes for tonight's game— a new pair of shoulder pads, a few more helmet straps—for this equipment was damaged in practice. Are they obliging and prompt? Do they meet your immediate needs? The key word which should help you decide where to purchase is *"service."* Will the establishment of your choice give you the best service? If so, your decision is a sound one.

In buying from one house you will incur the wrath of the other salespeople. Take your licking. You cannot satisfy all.

A word of caution to coaches who may wish to purchase outside of the community. It is a poor business policy. You should patronize local merchants whenever possible, for they are the people who support your teams as taxpayers and spectators.

RELATIONSHIP WITH THE PRESS

The relationship roster becomes significantly lengthened as the press is added to the list. The press is your mouthpiece. In turn, you and your team help them sell papers.

Dressing up factual information when reporting a game is left to the discretion of the person doing the reporting. He may write "Eisenhower High School defeated Paduca," or he may print, "Jim Bonder's Eisenhower Raiders defeated Paduca." The second type of reporting is an asset—a boost to every coach. Reporters keep you alive by placing you before the public. They allow your lights to shine by reporting on your team and you as a coaching personality.

Season Passes

In return for sports writers' kindness you can be of service to them. See to it that they have season passes admitting at least four people. The day before the game phone them about their need for tickets. They may wish to invite friends.

Reporters usually do not want a place on the bench, but if you run into a precocious newspaperman who desires to sit there, by all means allow him.

Give Him All the Details

Reporters need material to fill their allotted space. Give them whatever information they desire before or after a contest. They have a job to do, which happens to be reporting.

At times they second guess you by inquiring the reason for a certain strategic move. Do not resent them nor argue. Merely explain the reasons, theory, and assumption upon which you based your thinking. If you goofed and your strategy back-

fired—admit it. Inform the reporters that you erred. Tell them
the kids didn't lose the game, you did. An honest man is the
noblest work of God and the basis of high thinking.

Handling Reporters During Practice Sessions

When reporters visit your practice field, you should acknowl-
edge their presence immediately. Yell an enthusiastic greeting
so every member of your squad learns of your feelings toward
the press. Avoid a proprietary air when talking with them. Inflate their ego by interrupting your coaching to talk with him. If
you feel the need to explain what you are doing, do it with
enthusiasm. This is a fine time to huddle your squad and introduce the reporter to them.

There are times, however, when reporters unintentionally disrupt your practice schedule. If you are such a victim, solve your
problem in the following manner. Call the reporter inviting him
to a practice session of your choosing, ask him to lunch, or invite him to visit with you during a free period. If the reporter
understands the intricacies of your game, then go into details.
On the other hand, if his knowledge is limited, your explanation
should be elementary. Keep it simple and terse.

Give him a feeling of belonging, especially if he represents
the local press. Keep him informed by sharing intimate game
plans with him. Reporters are generally a fine lot. If you want
some incident held in strict confidence and not published, they
will be only too glad to comply. They seldom violate a
confidence.

An advantage of divulging your plans to a writer is the help
it provides him in reporting the game. He knows what to look
for. If by chance you change plans and fail to use a special play,
reporters will refrain from making mention of it in order that
you may use it in a future game.

The big cities have fifteen or twenty teams, which may lead
some readers to question the advisability of divulging your inner
secrets to reporters. Big cities are nothing more than a series of
neighborhoods, with one man assigned to a specific team. It is
his team to follow. If this is not the practice then of course the

closeness is missing. There is no need then to divulge your plans to the press.

However, more football is played in the outlying towns and boroughs than in the city, and it is those hundreds of little towns where the intimate relationship mentioned exists.

Newspapermen Are Prejudiced Fans

When you break it all down, newspapermen are nothing more than prejudiced fans who are rooting strongly for the home team. They are definitely partisan. Good teams need the press to stir the imagination of the fans. This fills the stadiums and arenas. Filled stadiums pay coaching salaries and buy fine equipment. In view of all this, it is easy to understand the importance of the press as representing a key strand in the web of relationship.

chapter four

PRODUCTIVE PRE-SEASON STAFF AND PLAYERS MEETINGS

The only things we ever keep are what we give away—LOUIS GINSBURG

Up to this point you have been concerned with the enlistment of outside agencies to help you strengthen your relationship with the players. The time has now arrived when you, as coach, must grapple personally with the problem. This phase of relationship cannot be delegated. This responsibility cannot be transferred. It is yours. In assuming this role you must carefully check all other contributions, for they are weathervanes pointing the direction you must take.

Through and to Players

Sport fans recognize the phrase "Tinker to Evers to Chance" as referring to the greatest double play combination in baseball history. In the same way, "Coach to Parent to Players" is the master stroke of school public relations. This three-fold relationship is the hub of your coaching success. It is common knowledge that if you have coaching know-how, plus confidence of the players and parents, you cannot miss.

You have spent considerable energy in developing absolute control over your players. It is now yours to use. In its implementation never exploit the players, but constantly strive to make them better citizens through the medium of athletic participation.

BECOMING ACQUAINTED MEETING

Arranging the Meeting

Whether this is your first session with the squad or the last one, meeting preparation and planning are a must. First you must have a justified reason for calling the meeting. One valid purpose is to stimulate and whet the squad's appetite for football participation.

Any youngster in attendance should have a ready answer to the question "Why was the meeting called?"

As coach, it is your responsibility to develop a meeting plan. I have experienced too many meetings convened and concluded with nothing accomplished for want of a basic plan. Evaluate your meetings by asking yourself, "Did I accomplish my mission?" "Was my purpose achieved?"

Staff Meeting Precedes Squad Meeting

It is wise to consult with your assistant coaches a week before planning a meeting. Ask them about a suitable time; one that will not inconvenience them too much. Assistants have academic duties and families that require their attention. You will not be very popular if you disrupt their basic duties.

Above all, be sure that all your assistants agree on every meeting agenda. The best practice in building a coaching team is to multiply your contacts with them. The worst calamity that can occur is to conduct a meeting and have your assistants disagree with your offensive and defensive strategy. Imagine what the players think when the coaching staff is in disagreement. The vital singleness of purpose is lost in confusion.

All this can be avoided if the head coach has a preliminary meeting with his staff. Every assistant deserves the courtesy of seeing the plans beforehand. Once your aides have been convinced, they reinforce the probability of the successful execution of your program. Early in my coaching career I suffered the ignominy of seeing a play unfold for the first time on the practice field—of seeing a new defensive maneuver for the first time in a practice scrimmage.

Each time you engage in this practice you are reducing your coaching years. I emphasize the importance of all coaches agreeing on the meeting plan long before it unfolds before the squad.

You must go to the meeting with the problem clearly in mind or written out. Introduce it briefly, then list the points to be covered in the ensuing discussion. Also list the questions to be raised, along with the possible conclusions to be reached. This is all done in a very subtle fashion and extreme care must be exercised.

At these staff meetings avoid a domineering attitude. Certainly you have an agenda in mind, but have it unfold gradually —do not cram it down your assistants' throats. This cautious procedure will tend to avoid any antagonism which in turn hinders total staff cooperation. Coaches who are too selfish to think of their co-workers never achieve the common purpose of group cooperation and unity. You must learn willingness to delegate authority without giving it away.

At the conclusion of the preliminary meeting with your assistants be sure to thank them for their time and cooperation. Tell them you are grateful for their help in ironing out any differences of opinion. Express your appreciation of their evaluation of coaching points and their willingness to compromise in order to arrive at a mutually satisfying conclusion—one which will help to spell success for the entire squad.

The Physical Environment—Footballarama

Physical arrangements for your meeting are important. If possible reserve a room in advance. Be sure there are enough chairs. A blackboard is a must, for it helps line up good ideas and is invaluable as a visual aid. The surroundings should denote football. Have a few footballs on the desk and I suggest you hold one in your hand as you talk to the men. Pictures of past school greats and famous stars old and new should be displayed prominently. If possible, try to create a football flavor by building a typical pigskin environment.

Meeting Notices

Every school should have a bulletin board and charge students with the responsibility of checking that board at least once every day. This practice, plus daily notice sheets, should keep students well informed on school activities. A notice of a football meeting should be posted on the official bulletin board at least one week in advance. Simultaneously with that posting should be the insertion of a similar announcement in the "Daily Gram." Constant repetition of this information right up to the day of the scheduled meeting is suggested.

An example of a meeting announcement follows:

> All candidates desiring to represent Roosevelt High School in football are requested to meet in room 107 at 2:30 Friday afternoon, May 19. The coaches will be on hand to welcome everyone—big, small, fat or skinny.
>
> Please come out and strive to be one of the chosen to wear the Blue and Gold.
>
> J. Jones, Coach

An additional meeting notice with an amusing flavor which I have successfully used follows:

> *Notice: Football Meeting*
> All men interested in breaking their necks please report to room 107 at 2:30 Friday, September 3, to meet the coaches.
>
> J. Jones, Coach

Meeting the Squad for the First Time

The initial meeting is one of first impressions. Your voice must have a commanding ring of definiteness, as if there is no doubt about the action and result you expect. As coach, you have prepared your agenda for this first meeting with the same deliberate care you use in preparing a lesson. The well defined objectives which you and your assistants established are ready to be presented to the squad. Specifically, those objectives are to have the squad recognize that you mean business, are fair, approachable, and friendly.

First, thank them for taking time out from so many other activities to attend your meeting. Inflate their egos by making them think they are doing you a favor.

Proceed then to give every candidate a mimeographed copy of the following:

What Does It Take To Be An Athlete?

Being an athlete does not imply merely wearing the uniform and being just a member of the squad. There are many more important phases to think about if you want to be a winner not only in football but in life as well. Your coaches want to impress you with the importance of the following qualities absolutely necessary for every good athlete.

1. *Are You Coachable?* Can you take coaching? Can you take criticism without ever looking for an alibi? Are you a "know it all?" Will you always do your level best to try to improve?

2. *Are you possessed with the spirit of competition which fires an intense desire to win?* Do you want to win with a passion—never taking "no" for an answer when there is a job to be done—a block to be made—a pass to be caught—a tackle to make? Does it bother you to lose?

3. *Are you willing to practice?*—not just reporting and putting in the necessary time but working every day with the same zeal, speed, and determination you use during a ball game? Do you have two speeds— a practice speed and a game speed? The greath athletes of the past were the ones who had one speed, and it was the same every day, every practice, every game. If you loaf and cheat in practice you will loaf and cheat in a ball game.

4. *Are you willing to make sacrifices?* Conditioning to play is not fun. It it not easy. It is stark punishment. Training is exacting; the responsibility is heavy. It is rough and includes personal denials in order to remain in tip-top condition, but it has its rewards. You thrill with an inner glow that reflects a feeling of happiness when your block springs a halfback through the line for a score. The only way for you

to remain in good shape is never to get out of it.

5. *Do you have an ardent desire to improve?* Are you willing to practice the things you cannot do three times longer than the things you can do? Are you willing to put in long grinding hours, concentrating on a skill until you perfected it? Are you eager to work so diligently at the skills you lack that they eventually become your strongest assets? We have seen too many men spend their time doing what they already do well. They never improved.

6. *Do you have the ability to think under fire?* Can you concentrate on the work to be accomplished at the moment? Can you shut out from your mind a previous failure, success, rule infraction, or personal insult in order to give undivided attention to the offensive and defensive maneuver in the here and now? Games are not won by yesterday's score, but by what is happening now, at this moment. Good athletes play every play up to the hilt—never depending on past success to aid them.

7. *Are you willing to be impersonal toward your opponents?* Do you shut out all personal feelings about your opponent except to hit him as hard, as often, and as quickly as you can, in accordance with the rules? Our experiences have taught us that the moment a player becomes personal he plays only to release individual grievances and ceases to play football as a team member.

8. *Do you believe in your school, your team, your coach?* Your school is as good as you make it. Your coach is a genuine employee of your school given the responsibility of coaching, not his team, but your team. Are you willing to work toward that spirit of oneness so that everyone possesses the feeling of belonging through their contributions? Will you keep uppermost in mind that when a coach blisters the team with criticism his remarks are never meant to be personal affronts? The only intent is to pressurize you to want to rectify your omissions so that success for all results. Despite his scathing censure he loves all of you as if you were his very own.

9. *Are you willing to study just as hard as before coming out for football?* Football was never meant to take the place of studies. The athletic tail must never

wag the academic dog. This involves a realignment
in your time schedule. If football will consume two
hours of your day then you must draw time not
from your scholastic program but from hours previously devoted to personal pursuits. If you must
eliminate something from your schedule it must not
be study time. First things come first, and your
academic growth is of paramount importance.

10. *Will you strive daily to improve your muscular coordination and speed?* Football is a game of move-
ment and daily drills will tend to speed up your reaction time. Speed and coordination are necessary
ingredients in a winning combination. Only through
hard work can improvement here be realized. Those
of you who lack these two physical qualities can find
a place on the team by improving in other attributes.

Yours, in sport,
The Coaches

Ask your candidates to go home and read and reread this
message. If possible, have them place it on their bedroom walls.
If they are willing to comply to the best of their abilities with
the ten requisites, then you want them on your squad.

It would be wise for you to put a copy of this communique
on the bulletin board in the squad's dressing room. Keeping
material of this nature constantly before them will pay dividends.

Your Coaching Philosophy Unfolds

If you assume coaching duties in a school already the posses-
sor of a fine athletic record, tell the squad your reason for coming
to them as coach is because you believe in the continuation of
their excellent work. If the school has a poor athletic record, impress upon them the feasibility of improving their lot. You believe in the school, and anyone not sharing that devotion should
leave.

As a coach, you will be as good as the squad wants you to
be; and they as good as they make each other.

Tell them "As a team you must strive to be a unifying force
in school spirit by creating a feeling of oneness."

Stress the fact that you did not accept the responsibility of coaching Roosevelt High with the intent of losing games. You expect to win them all, and lose with grace only to superior teams. To achieve that objective, all must give unsparingly of themselves. Unlimited individual effort is a requisite which will crystallize into team effort. There is no greater thrill than occurs when a group of individuals suddenly becomes a team. Be emphatic about demanding this relationship. Your sport requires sacrifices and if any refuse to make them—ask them to turn in their uniforms, and you will remain friends. "I want you to play as if you are afraid to lose." You insist always on 100 per cent effort. Nothing short of perfection will satisfy. Trifles make perfection but perfection is no trifle. Let me illustrate.

Centuries ago, someone discovered the zero. The zero means *"nothing"* but this *"nothing"* was a world shaking factor. Without the zero you could never conceive the one, the two, etc.

Impress the squad with this statement, "I will not stand for a losing team."

You want a high level of performance always, but you will never ask the unreasonable. You are not interested solely in undefeated teams; however, you are concerned with out-fundamentalizing opponents. Once you out-fundamental other teams, outscoring them takes care of itself. Invariably, it will follow automatically.

There are four necessary ingredients for the development of successful football and these essentials should be stressed every day of the season. None of them is romantic. The coaching staff assumes that every member of the squad knows nothing:

> "We plan to start from the ground up. We have detailed fundamentals that fit our style of play. We believe in them, and if any of you have been taught differently we expect to reshape you to fit our scheme. Regardless of your years of experience, you will begin by perfecting the stance; the starting point of a brand new man. Anyone not interested in perfecting these four basic fundamentals which follow is not our type of ball player. We do not want him.
> "The four fundamentals are:
> 1. Blocking.

2. Tackling.
3. Speed.
4. Communication.

"The first three are not new. They have been requisites since the inception of the game. The fourth element *"Communication"* is the added feature of the modern era. In fact, it is the essence and heart of the popular "T" formation.

"Together we shall strive to develop these four facets of the game. There exists a high positive correlation between the successful execution of these basic essentials and the number of games won. Teams well versed in these principles very seldom have losing seasons. We do not want to lose. Of course we realize that we cannot win every game, but we insist on winning a minimum of fifty per cent.

"Despite our ardent desire for victory, winning is not the sole objective of football. However, it remains one of the primary objectives of the game, otherwise they could not keep score.

"A player is under a moral obligation to do everything he possibly can do to win—anything else is cheating. If you lose because your effort has compelled the other fellow to beat you—if you have forced him to prove he is better—then—and only then—you can lose, because you have done so with dignity.

"In order that a team which loses has not played in vain, football must have a residual value. That value is learning to lose—learning to bounce back after failure—seeking the cause of failure, and being determined to do something about it."

We believe in winning—that all-out effort should be exerted to finish first. But it is the striving, not necessarily the arriving, that brings out the best in a man. Some good must result in the attempt a team makes to win. Winning is merely one result of that attempt. There must be a complement to that win, which naturally accrues to the team which also made the attempt but lost.

In this age of satellites the net result of a football game is as unimportant, as insignificant, as one flake of snow falling on this huge earth of ours.

If you had visited Main Street anywhere in the U.S.A. 17 years ago, you would have seen an 18-year old boy in the uniform of his country. You might have watched him write a tender letter to his mother; written as if his pen were dipped in his very heart's blood. If you had looked again, you would have noticed a youngster with an empty sleeve hanging from his shoulder, and another standing on an artificial leg. Had you looked further, you would have seen the lifeless body of another boy brought home. His was the supreme sacrifice. He was fairer in death than Adonis, over whom the Goddess of Beauty wept. You would have watched them bury him in the churchyard, under the green grass where his little feet roamed in childhood.

These men lost so that others could win, but their attempts to reach victory—to win—was never lost. It was constantly before them and uppermost in their minds. In fact, if they were to repeat their experiences, their original intent would not vary—the seeking of victory.

Since so much has been written about winning, the preceding may seem incongruous to the reader. I do not mean to appear inconsistent. What I have torn asunder, I have sought to join together because winning and losing are basic to playing the game. It is impossible to approach the ultimate result of the game in a piecemeal fashion.

Enthusiasm Caught, Not Taught

As you talk to your squad your enthusiasm becomes contagious. You start an epidemic. Impress them with the fact that you are soaked in football—you love it with a passion. You eat —sleep—dream it. Fan your glow into a real flame and hope some of it rubs off on them.

Inform them that there will be times during the season when their backs will be to the goal posts. Their breathing will become labored, saliva will be heavy and lumpy. Each one will experience a mouth filled with cotton. They will be dirty, sweaty and tired—but they dare not quit. A winner never quits and a quitter never wins.

Tell them, "Ten years from now you will reminisce and relive all the moments of glory achieved during your playing days."

The 1957 West Chester College team had an undefeated season. Years from now the many touchdowns they scored will be forgotten but the goal line stand during the Bloomsburg game, which made the unblemished record possible, will long be remembered, because it was a true team effort.

Tell your squad that when they have passed their last exam and triumphantly exhibit their ribboned diplomas, their link with the past will not be games won, but instead, how they played the game.

Ego-Submission

Within each of us there are certain personality characteristics which tend to prevent complete cooperation.

As we rid ourselves of such traits tolerance is required. Only by exercising patience will these obstacles disappear and a team effort result.

As a coach, I must point out some typical destructive qualities that hamper every ball club. There is antagonism, jealousy, buck-passing, and fear of being overshadowed and losing the limelight. To be a team member, one must condition himself to subdue these natural instincts. It is like the case of the outfielder who makes four miraculous catches to win for his pitcher, and then receives no credit. It is the pitcher who makes the headlines. Yet without the other *eight* men a pitcher could *never begin* to imagine a victory. Individual contributions of every team member are taken for granted the moment a player puts on his headgear to play the game.

No Shortcuts

In football there are no short cuts. The path to victory and glory is paved with hard work. To have eleven men execute a play perfectly requires exact cooperation—this can be achieved only through constant practice.

The great pianist, Paderewski, attained greatness because he practiced morning noon, and night. His friends became alarmed over his failing health and begged him to take a month off. The artist replied, "No." They suggested a week—again he replied, "No." They would compromise for even a day's rest. Again the response, "No." "If I do not practice for one day, I become aware of it. If I do not practice for two days my friends become aware of it, and if I do not practice for three days my enemies become aware of it." Thus was a great career carved out of sheer persistent hard work.

Years ago I had a guard with limited ability comparable to the other guard candidates yet this young man started every game and played longer. He lived on the field. There were days when I had to order him into the shower. He would work untiringly to perfect skills in which he was weak. When I talked to him he said, "Coach, if I can pull out one second faster, our 36 play will be more successful." Before the season ended our 36 play was our most consistent gainer, thanks to the hard work of the guard.

Everyone Starts from Scratch

You must make clear to your squad the fact that everyone will be starting from scratch. This cannot be obviated. They must be told that it doesn't make any difference as to who they are or whether their hair is curly or straight. Each player has to produce to play on the varsity. You have no favorites—no fraternities. Your eleven best men will make up the first team regardless of nationality, creed, color, financial status or social prominence. In order to give life and encouragement to the smaller candidates it will be necessary for you to impress the squad that you do not intend to select the team on the basis of weight and speed alone. These qualities are important only if possessed by a man with game courage, spirit, and discipline. Tell them you want men who will rise to the level of a tough situation. Remind them of little men, such as Davey O'Brien of the Philadelphia Eagles, and Eddie Le Baron of the Washington Redskins. These men were little potatoes but hard to peel. Their hearts are bigger than their bodies.

I remember a little guard named Bill Berrardelli on our 1954-

57 squads who weighed in at 165 lbs. He was not well-coordinated but he was a stubborn defensive player. He was all "guts" and grit, but much too little to anchor a college line. I thought "If I have to go with him I'm not going to develop a line that will help win a lot of ball games." We had another guard, much bigger and faster, and I decided to play him.

In our game against Youngstown University things were going rough, so I put Bill into the game just to rest the bigger man. Our defense immediately improved, and the entire team seemed to be infused with new life. Youngstown's successful plays up the middle were stopped. Bill Berrardelli became a fixture as left guard for the remainder of the year.

Plans for the following year convinced me that the position of left guard would be our weakness, so I practically ignored Bill in the pre-season practice and concentrated on the bigger men.

After the first ball game, I decided that physically superior men are not always the answer. Berrardelli believed in himself. He never stopped trying even after he had convinced me he was the man for the job.

In 1955 our first string center was injured. A highly recommended high school product whose size made him an ideal candidate for the job was our second string center. I immediately began to ready him to replace the varsity center. Three days before the game the big man broke his shoulder in a scrimmage. I was compelled to reach down into my third stringers and bring up a slender 160 lb. man named Dick Borkowski, who lacked the desired height as well as weight.

The only reason for starting him in the Drexel game was that he was the only center left. That game was only five minutes old when my entire evaluation of Borkowski changed. He was all over the field. Not only did he run the first string center out of a job, but the big high school product never played. His heart wasn't big enough.

If you feel these examples have not put your point across, emphasize your desire to have men with the drive and "guts" of little Nellie Fox, the second baseman of the Chicago White Sox.

He is the smallest man on any Big League roster, but he is the most respected competitor in America. Fox is supposed to have said to a reporter who inquired why he didn't rest more, "If I rest, I rust."

Emphasize this aspect to your men and say, "I want men who love contact—men who feel the compulsion to bang heads." I have known men, cut from our college squad, who loved to play so much that they went out looking for semi-professional teams to join.

Their Academic Program

Announce to your squad that you will not tolerate any man on your squad who fails to respect faculty authority and refuses to work scholastically. It takes courage to study and play ball. You do not want players lacking in this type of courage. You want men who will not neglect their studies. The scholastic program takes precedence in your eyes. Under no condition do you plan to change your philosophy in this regard.

Introducing Your Assistants

Make part of the agenda the introduction of your assistant coaches. Their presentation must be in flowering glowing terms. It would be wise to mention some outstanding achievement in their background as you introduce them. You leave no doubt about your conviction that these helpers are the greatest athletic minds in the world. This glorification will be reflected and bounce back two-fold. Allow them to speak if they so desire. In so doing you buy cooperation of able men, with whom you plan to join hands, doing things you cannot do alone.

Divulging Your Plans

Time is then taken briefly to reveal your system of play and seasonal organization plans. At this time you merely mention the general techniques you intend to employ in order to meet the schedule. A word about teams on your schedule would be appropriate at this time. The revealing of all the intricate details of the plan will be held in abeyance until the pre-seasonal meetings are held.

It would be timely to show a film of one of your better games. Certainly you edit the film beforehand in order that it will have a lifting influence on their evaluation of your ability. Only a fool would use a film not reviewed and spliced to show the better plays. This is not deception, merely good salesmanship. Television commercials never bring the liabilities of their products before the public. Why should you?

Offer Them Your Time—Get Them into Your Home

Your squad must be led to believe that they can call on you at any time, either at home or in your office. Your time is their time. Insist they come to you with scholastic and personal problems as well as athletic. Make sure there is in your home an abundance of pretzels, cookies, candy and cokes. Your living room should be replete with football literature, and included in this literature should be your scrap book. They will eventually find it and learn of your accomplishments.

Your squad members become your adopted children and you accord them similar treatment. In my early high school coaching, my home was open-house seven days a week. It would often become necessary to chase the youngsters nightly, in order that they would receive the proper rest. We found in each other's company warmth, confidence and mutual trust.

When players are visiting your home, removed from the tension of the practice field, you have the opportunity to do some coaching. In some instances more coaching can be realized in these informal home gatherings than on the field.

During this getting-acquainted period and at informal home meetings, guard against players becoming too friendly and carelessly intimate. Provide against a change in your social status by insisting the players use "Mr." or "Coach" before your name.

Connie Mack managed the Philadelphia Athletics for 52 years. In that time he coached many outstanding teams, and those of his players who reached stardom are too numerous to mention by name. Every member of his team always called him Mr. Mack. No one would dare address him by his first name. Before the late Al Simmons died I spoke to him for approximately an hour about Connie Mack. Al was 54 years old and had left the Athletics nearly three years prior. Despite the span of time he still referred to him as *"Mr. Mack."* I inquired about the handle. Simmons said, "Mr. Mack is the only way I can talk about him. He had too much dignity to be called 'Connie' by his players. We never even gave it a thought. The 'Mr.' came naturally."

You will find much emulation by your players. In light of this, your appearance, dress, voice, and your leadership must be such that you are worthy of their attention.

Terminating the Meeting

Again take time to thank your assistants and the squad for their attendance. Be sincere in stating that you hope this will be the first link in a long chain of successes.

You explain to the squad that at the end of the season you should be able to look into each other's eyes and not be ashamed. You and they are going to cross the years together, and you want to make permanent friends. Athletic history is found where you make it. Ask them to join you so together you will add pages of glory to the history of their high school.

BUILDING AND MAINTAINING
EFFECTIVE TEAM DISCIPLINE

The best preacher is the heart, the best teacher is time, the best book is the world, and the best judge is God——CARL SANDBURG

Chapter 1 was designed to show the peculiar relationship that encompasses the player and the coach. A major portion of that relationship evolves from discipline. Despite discipline being the keynote of that earlier section, this chapter will go into a detailed interpretation of that essential. How it is secured, maintained, and the techniques involved, will be discussed.

An auxiliary purpose of this chapter is to offer the coach an explanation of the basic philosophy behind the strange discipline he must exact. It has been my experience that all coaches employ disciplining devices, but many lack the ability to understand or explain how or why.

A logical clarification of the technique that coaches emphasize during the season but have never been consciously aware of will be presented. This will enable you to explain to the entire world why you are compelled to do certain things. If you wish to rationalize your deeds—the contents which follows will supply the necessary material.

I am fully aware that some who inhabit the "ivory tower" will take exception to this approach, but stark realism must not give way to any maudlin sentimentality. I am by compulsion urged to write truth and not lose myself in utopian idealism, because I have never met with nor read of a good team which lacked discipline.

Discipline a Mystery

At the outset it is important to realize that there is no one formula for discipline. It is a composition of many elements—all must be articulated. Complicating matters is the mystery surrounding these component parts. They are most difficult to recognize. If the ingredients are missing one immediately becomes aware of their absence. If they are present, the mystery is heightened because one has difficulty giving them identity.

At this point you may be confused and flustered. Perhaps additional lines may unravel the thread.

At best, discipline is like a girl on a date. She receives as much respect as she demands and not one bit more. It is like puppets on strings. You let out string as long as they are performing exactly as you wish. The moment one attempts to take the string away from you—you give a hard yank to remind the erring puppet that he is still in your charge.

Discipline Defined

Discipline is a by-product of good coaching. It is a relationship established by the coach which elicits from players the type of response that leads to successful playing conditions. It is a rough process of helping players adjust to a special environment.

Fear As a Component

Despite the difficulty encountered in pinpointing the ingredients of discipline, one ingredient does emerge quite clearly. This component is fear. Not physical fear, but fear of losing something a player wants and covets. The fact that the "have-nots" want what the "haves" have, makes fear a healthy sign. Punishment has its inception in fear. Punishment is not revenge, but only a means of instilling fear of the consequences, in order that a player does not indulge in rule infractions.

Specifically, the player's fear is that he will not play. Nature provides the coach with an assist here, for a condition exists when more players are competing for less playing positions. The ratio is usually 40-11. Forty players competing for only eleven positions. A victory of the few over the many is constantly present.

The oddity here is that players actually derive pleasure in participating in this relationship, which the rules of the game have forced upon them. The person in control of this natural situation is the coach, who enjoys the sole right to decide which eleven men will play at a given time. Fear of not being in the starting lineup, added to the fear of not playing at all, is in itself sufficient as a tool of discipline. Punishment here does not hurt, it humiliates all those who do not play. The ego of a good player cannot tolerate humiliation.

If the word "fear" arouses an ugly connotation in the minds of some, perhaps the author should write that the essence of love is fear. Fear of losing the one you love. If you do not experience that fear, then perhaps the only reason you have her is because no one else wanted her.

Group Therapy

Life as a participant of a team is actually life in a crowd. The same old crowd, day in and day out. Someone must control the team exactly as some controlling element directs every crowd. No squad can live together in close proximity during the season without rules and leadership. The group is the frame of reference and the coach directs that reference. Discipline cannot lose out to self-expression. A group therapy must emerge. Players are permanently under this effective control. A group learns to obey authority, behave honorably, and maintain good order not only because the members feel forced to do so, but because they choose to do so. They have been helped to realize that these modes of behavior are essential for winning teams.

A coach's lot is made easier because control is inherent in

group-centered activity, which results in a common aim shared by the group. The aim of winning dominates the interests of all squad members, and makes the achievement of the individual who supports that objective greeted by group acclaim. Flouting the will of the group results in loss of acceptance.

Good Discipline Results in Squad Mentacide

From the time your invitation letter summons players to report for practice, they become your charge to do your bidding. Your correspondence must set the keynote for the entire season. It establishes the central purpose of playing each play of every game up to the hilt. Players are indentured to a principle without a contract. Everything you undertake in your practice is aimed to result in your squad committing mentacide. You mechanize the squad's mental processes so that they conform to your own thinking. When this is accomplished, your players will without question give ready acceptance to obedience. Obedience is not weakness bowing to strength, but rather, submission to trained authority. The harmony and efficiency of the entire ball club is dependent on compliance. True obedience does not anger or dispute; neither does it delay or murmur. It goes to work immediately to fulfil the coaching commands. It is Pavlovian conditioning at its best.

The Encyclopedia Britannica relates a striking example of prompt, unquestioning obedience in the Charge of the Light Brigade during the Crimean War. "A series of engagements between the Russians and the English took place in the little town of Balaclava on October 25, 1854. The Russians were for a time victorious and threatened the English-held port. The English attack was directed by General Scarlett. Then through a misunderstanding of the orders of Lord Raglan, the Commander in Chief, Lord Cardigan was directed to charge the Russian artillery at the northern extremity of the Balaclavian Valley with the Light Brigade. Lord Cardigan was exceedingly unpopular as an officer but no sooner was the order given than this Light Brigade hewed its way past the Russian guns and routed the enemy cavalry. Of the six hundred and seventy horsemen who made the charge only one hundred and ninety-eight returned. As an act of war it was madness, but as an act of soldierly obedience, it was sublime."

Another example of blind obedience is found in tales of the Japanese soldiers whose devotion to their country was so intense that they stuck to their lonely island posts years after the war ended, as if the Emperor were still looking at them.

If you have that type of discipline, your players will find love and faith in surrendering their individual thinking to your thinking. The fact that all think the same gives them a share and a feeling of belonging. Through this group action every individual's self esteem will be increased.

Field Discipline Leads to Self-Control

Discipline on the field will manifest itself in self-control later in life. This transfer is made possible because the moment a player yields to his impulses he gives up his right to play. Self-control requires courage. There is nothing more discouraging than a player who is not his own master. During a close game when the going is touch and go, players tire and become prone to anger; only the well-balanced will obey the rules. Good discipline practiced every day enables players to keep a grip upon themselves regardless of pressure.

Edison had this discipline when he worked on the phonograph. In his repeated efforts to make the phonograph reproduce a certain sound he said, "From eighteen to twenty hours a day I have worked on the single word, 'specia.' I have said into the machine the word specia—specia—specia, but the instrument responded, pecia—pecia—pecia. It was enough to drive one mad but I held firm and succeeded." Self control won the day for him.

In 1947, West Chester was a participant in the Burley Bowl, played in Johnson City, Tennessee. During the third quarter we were leading, 21-7, and our opponent resorted to some uncalled-for fisticuffs. One of our finest tackles entered the game, reported to the referee, and was suddenly punched in the face. There was nothing wrong with the lineman's courage. He merely knew he was more valuable in the game than on the bench. It was gratifying to see him ride the blow, then walk away. This gave me more personal satisfaction than winning the game. Of course, the game was won on blocking and tackling, but self-control helped too. Players with more courage than common sense will be a detriment to your team. It takes more guts to turn away than fight. Some one once said, "Love your enemies; it will drive them crazy."

In the summer of 1938 I attended a baseball game at Shibe Park and encountered my college football coach, Marty Brill. Two years had elapsed since my last college game, and graduation. As I was leaving the park, I lit a cigar. When I suddenly caught sight of my college coach, instinctively I dropped the cigar and stepped on it. I just could not smoke and be comfortable in his presence. He laughed at me, offered me a fresh cigar and held his lighter to it. This was ample proof of real discipline made a permanent part of my life.

Conformity Is Not Surrender

Some critics have attacked the coach's demand of ready conformity and docility of players as nothing more than a police action. They point out that this type of discipline breaks down the minute the coach leaves the field for the suppressed energies of the players breaks forth into acts of misbehavior. They actually believe that the only time players train is when they are under the direct surveillance of a policeman. The fallacy of this assumption can be seen on every playing field of America where young men begin a training program of their own weeks before the opening of school. A second refutation is in evidence on the day of the game. The coach is not near them, in fact, he is fifty yards removed yet the attitudes and behavior of the players are exemplary.

Players who are conditioned to accept control imposed by the coach usually develop into good citizens. Living day by day means accepting controls; in fact, it is a requirement of our society. Clothes must be hung; cars operate on streets, not pavements; cars housed in garages, not living rooms; lunch eaten at stated times; classes change with the bell, and property and traffic regulations obeyed. Everywhere we turn there are regulations, and most are not of our making. If we accept transfer of training, then society benefits from a coach's insistence on players subscribing to his edicts.

New Type Discipline Must Be Learned

Previous to reporting for football, a player's source of disciplinary control is found largely in his loyalty to his parents. It is the opinion of many sociologists today that parental discipline has decayed, and new adjustments are necessary. When a player reports for football, his efforts to become accepted by his team are based on loyalty to individuals. It must be broadened to include group control and restraints. The squad comprises that group, with standard responses being established by the coach and accepted by the players. A mutual benefit results from this arrangement; first, the coach receives the complete cooperation of his players, secondly, players develop habits of self control that lead to effective citizenship.

As coach, it is imperative that you remember that this type of behavior must be learned. You are responsible for showing errant players the proper way of doing things. This makes the punishment wholesome and prevents a repetition of the offense. Good discipline not only teaches what not to do, but what to do. Players must be instructed that obeying the rules is more rewarding than flouting them. Their reward is manifested by being singled out for one of the eleven starting assignments. When this condition has been achieved, players have entered the advanced stage of self-discipline.

ORGANIZATION THE BASIS OF DISCIPLINE

Organization is the most basic tool of discipline. It is the heart of discipline. Players respect a coach who comes on the field with a demeanor that offers evidence that he knows his stuff. He has a schedule of practice which insures the systematic progress of all players engaged. So strongly does the coach believe in this pattern that he will not tolerate any disruption in the planned program of the day. Flexibility exists only in a limited degree in order to compensate for individual differences; in fact, pre-planning practically renders this nil.

Good organization means assigning every coach and every manager to a specific duty to be executed in a clearly defined method. Method rules every department of play. There is no talent like method. All the necessary material such as different colored jerseys, markers, and first aid kit must be on hand. I have witnessed the failure of many practices because of poor organization. I recall a coach who had his men all pepped up to begin an intra-squad scrimmage, and suddenly discovered the jerseys were not out. This cooling-off period and lack of planning takes the edge off everything. The worst calamity to befall a squad is the coach who fails to have the first aid kit out every day. This omission endangers the safety of every player. There is no acceptable excuse for this. Well disciplined coaches and teams have everything planned so that the squad's drills move like clockwork. Nothing is trial and error.

It would help if a list of material needed daily was given to the managers. This would augment the coaching schedule discussed earlier and produce a completely efficient organization.

My experience has also taught me to spend considerable time in early practice teaching the skills players need, plus the procedures to develop them. This enables players to go ahead independently practicing these phases while you are concentrating on other men. This initial help enables players to develop themselves through their own continued efforts even when not supervised. Players very seldom become discouraged under this arrangement. If your coaching personnel is limited to two or three men this procedure is a must.

The Test of Good Discipline

There are many hallmarks of a well disciplined team. They are in evidence during practices and during games. Good discipline is manifested during practice sessions in the following manner:

1. Squad possesses fruitful study habits.
2. Squad believes in school.

3. Squad believes in coach.
4. Squad believes in teammates.
5. Squad is punctual for practices and meetings.
6. Squad trains faithfully.
7. Squad dresses properly.
8. Squad hustles every minute.
9. Squad respects its community.
10. Squad members act as personal ambassadors of the school.

During a game, discipline is evidenced by:

1. Being on time.
2. Dressing neatly and remaining so throughout the game.
3. Carrying out coaches' orders whether the squad agrees with them or not.
4. Maintaining emotional stability in the face of failure or hostile spectators.
5. Accepting officials and their decisions as part of the game.
6. Once the game is played refraining from passing derogatory remarks concerning the opponent.

The West Chester team practices at 3 P.M. every day unless players have classes. All candidates are expected to be on the field ready to go at that time. A man reporting late is sent in with the request that he report on time tomorrow. If the player cares he will be on time. If he does not care he will not help you anyway, and you are better off without him.

Our 1957 undefeated West Chester team was well disciplined. This was obvious during one of our scrimmages when we were experiencing difficulty running our bread and butter off-tackle play. Coach Killinger asked in exasperation, "What the hell's wrong here?" Seven linemen answered in unison, "My fault, coach." We knew who was at fault, but it was heartwarming to notice such discipline.

The 1957 Cleveland Browns were a fine, disciplined team, which is a tribute to their great coach, Paul Brown. Just before their game with the Philadelphia Eagles, the Browns registered at the Warwick Hotel in Philadelphia. They were as well dressed as anyone present in the lobby, and could easily have passed for business men attending an important convention. Lunch was at 12:15, and by 12:15 every one of them was seated at the table. No stragglers. This is typical of how Coach Brown's discipline manifests itself on and off the field.

BEST DISCIPLINE BY INDIRECTION

The finest discipline I have experienced in my twenty years of coaching resulted from winning the affection of my players. Love can be the instrument for forging this devotion to you. Cheerful obedience is one of the strongest proofs of this love.

Every member of the 1932-36 La Salle College football squad loved our coach, Marty Brill. Just a word from him; a kind word, did so much when it was uttered in public or private. To learn that we had pleased him pleased us in turn. When we had displeased him, it displeased us, in fact it gnawed at our inners.

Marty Brill possessed a magnetic personality which filled us with self-confidence. He was fair. He employed ridicule and sarcasm in the hope of obtaining a better effort from candidates who had the ability but were not putting out. He never used these techniques on a sensitive player who fell short despite giving it all he had all the time.

We identified ourselves with him in order to borrow some of his fortitude. He was many things and often they contradicted each other. He utilized paternal concern, relieved us of any sense of guilt when we lost, yet at times was a tyrant. The oddity is that we loved him completely for his strength, regardless of the role he was enacting.

I vividly recall an early meeting in which Coach Brill discussed the importance of training rules. After sowing these seeds he suddenly turned the meeting over to the captain, admonishing him to obtain from the squad those rigid training rules which would govern them. In those days I thought we were ruling ourselves. Today I see his technique with a finer understanding.

STRENGTHENING INTER-SCHOOL DISCIPLINE

In the course of playing traditional rivals year in and year out, the rivalry frequently gets out of hand. More often than not the spectators' interest is responsible for this condition. Good coaches take remedial steps to combat this eventuality. Those that fail to take these precautions experience a severance of game relationships.

Techniques to strengthen inter-school relationships may be achieved through exchange assemblies or a dance following the game, plus coaching remarks just prior to the game.

Exchanging coaches and captains during assembly programs in which sportsmanship is emphasized will be a big contribution.

Stimulating the home team to sponsor an inter-school dance the night of the game is another technique utilized with success. A joint committee chosen from squad members of both schools cements harmony.

As coach you can help by reminding your players before the game that the visiting players are your guests and you insist they be treated as such. You want the game played hard; giving no quarter and asking none, but always within the sphere of the rules.

COACHING DISCIPLINE IS UNIQUE

In comparing teacher–pupil relationship in the classroom with coach–player relationship on the athletic field, one discovers many similarities and a few marked variances. The most obvious and glaring contrast lies in knack of disciplining. Contrary to popular opinion, rules which apparently function well when applied in the classroom are rendered impotent when employed on the field. There are eleven basic reasons for this difference:

1. Build, not relieve, tension.
2. Group participation.
3. Demands unnatural.
4. No share in planning.
5. Coach is czar.

    6. Competitive dissatisfaction.
    7. Evaluation.
    8. Need for immediate results.
    9. A select group.
  10. Football discipline is constant.
  11. Drills a must.

Build, Not Relieve, Tension

In the classroom and in the outside world, people spend money to get rid of tension. Exhibit A of this is the millions of dollars spent yearly on tranquilizers and "happy pills." In the public eye, tension is harmful bacteria. We are plied with commercials guaranteeing us relaxation and sleep. In football the opposite is true—here you create a high level of tension and momentum. A coach fosters tensions and anxieties to accomplish the task at hand.

I have witnessed young men whose emotional reactions to the loss of a loved one were not as overt as those experienced over a defeat suffered by their respective schools.

I have seen players become so engrossed in playing that it appeared a real life and death struggle with honor and all at stake. The hotter the battle the more a player's body glows with physical exaltation and nerves that thrill to the impact of body meeting body.

Group Participation

Football is a game apart. It is the only game where a massed group is engaged in every moment of play through physical contact. In other sports, one or two players alone can complete a play with no contact, as a pitcher and catcher—but not in football. In the classroom, instruction continues despite the inattention of one or two students. In football, one missed assignment is fatal.

Demands Unnatural

Because football is a different type of work demanding self-punishment, a maximum of external policing and pressures is a must. As coach, you must keep uppermost in mind that what you require a player to do is foreign in forces of nature. It is contrary to everything else he does—contrary to the way he spends his other time and activities.

In other endeavors, if he tires, he sits—not in football. He wants to play despite fatigue, injury, and pain. If he is thirsty and hungry he eats—not in football for here his life follows a rigid schedule. If he is dirty and sweaty he washes—not in football—for he is compelled to wait until the coach sends him in.

In view of these factors, you cannot allow players to discipline themselves. The freer, more informal type of discipline known as self-management, and popularized within the last quarter of a century, is ineffective in athletics. Players have had no training experience nor have they the maturity to assume this obligation. Someone must supply the control that players cannot supply themselves. As a coach, you cannot permit them to pursue their own inclinations. Only chaos can accrue from the current theory of "permissiveness." Individuality must succumb to conformity. Players always respect a coach who is a real "take charge guy."

No Share in Planning

"Take time but hurry, hurry" is the theme of this variance. As coach you are constantly making quick decisions, because you just do not have a large cushion of time. Players seldom choose their activity; as coach, you are constantly manipulating them to make your decisions. Your training, and their lack of it qualify you to do that, just as doctors and lawyers make solitary decisions. Teachers may share planning with pupils because learning could be fun. Football is not play, it is drudgery. In fact, coaches wonder in amazement how players can take it all. Good discipline is a painful and irksome ordeal, and the longer a player can stand it, the better person he will be.

Coach a Czar

Discipline on the field places the coach in a position of being a tyrant, dictator, and czar. The coach at once is a lawmaker, accuser, prosecutor, judge, and executive. The coach is the last judgment. There is no higher appeal. Players are helpless in the coach's hands, for he convicts, sentences, and holds the power of reprieve and pardon. As coach, however, never abuse the power so that you lose a player's respect. Experience has taught me that if this force is used judiciously, respect for the coach grows. If this power is abused, coaches will discover that injudicious words and actions will return like the ghost of Hamlet's father to haunt them.

I want to point out that I believe this rigid discipline has been a key factor in keeping the basic decency of players indestructible.

Competitive Dissatisfaction

In this day, competition is milder in the classroom than on the athletic field. On the football field a coach not only creates competitive forces but adds a new twist known as competitive dissatisfaction. This may appear distasteful, but in coaching parlance it is really a desirable quality. Players should come out of a game unhappy and griping continuously that they do not play enough. Competition to play must be so keen that men in every position hate to see some one come in to replace them for fear they will be outdone. Coaches realize that this manifests itself into a supreme effort on the part of every man. Players must be convinced of a coach's willingness to make changes the minute one's performance is sub par. The oddity here is that the players derive pleasure from participating in the very forces of competition which often produce ugly results.

Evaluation

Teachers have visitors occasionally. Teachers are not exposed to the public. They ordinarily teach thirty or less pupils at one sitting. The coach, on the other hand, is exposed to as many as 5,000 spectators all sitting in critical judgment. Teachers are not exposed to the severe evaluation of the public; as a result, they can relax and concentrate only on a portion of the taxpayers' children. The coach, besides looking after the charges of the taxpayers, is exposed to everyone else at large. This difference in evaluation places undue pressure on the coach and he must resort to special techniques to combat it. Teaching is not a crisis, but winning a game is.

In football you constantly weigh the task players have elected to do and whether or not it has been accomplished. Personalities are divorced from any measuring rod. Only results are coldly appraised. Effort on the field that has failed to convert itself into success is ignored completely. On the other hand, effort in the classroom is associated with the personality and invariably receives some recognition. When failure occurs in the classroom some remedial steps are taken to overcome it. On the field, however, failure must be replaced with immediate success. Remedial steps are taken but the change in personnel is of necessity a swift one.

Need for Immediate Results

When a pupil is having difficulty in the classroom, measures are taken to investigate his background, to find the cause of the deviation. The principal, guidance counsellors, and the school psychiatrist work with parents as a team to overcome the student's problem. In athletics, results must be in the here and now —there is no time to find out "why" and negotiate, reason, or compromise. As coach, you are interested only in immediate results. You are not a junior psychiatrist. Time does not permit a diligent search into causes; while you are investigating, the season is ending on a disastrous note. Therefore, you are required to establish a certain pattern of behavior and anything that deviates from that is misbehavior that must be punished so it does not happen again. Punishment is swift and manifests itself with removal from the game or being cut outright from the squad. Personal feelings are never a criterion in judging a player. You judge only the results; who supplies them is immaterial.

As coach, you are justified in registering impatience over excuses for jobs undone. You will tire hearing sad stories and rationalizations on the part of players. If this sounds tough, it is because I know the excuses and the answers to the excuses.

A Select Group

The moment a player draws his uniform he becomes a member of a select school group. He now takes on a special mantle which singles him out as a student with membership in an elite group. As a member of the squad he realizes playing is a road to importance and a form of worthy achievement. On the field, he hungers for success with a motivation somewhat keener than that which he exhibits in the classroom. It is important to keep in mind that there are forces which compel him to attend class. There is compulsory attendance legislation in every state in America. In football, he elects to compete, and there is never any compulsion.

If there does exist any binding force, it stems from his desire to obtain recognition from the public, plus the feeling that he possesses talents worthy of the respect of others. This desire, he realizes, can be fulfilled faster as a member of a team than as an individual. Players will only receive more for themselves by getting the most for the team.

Football Discipline Is Constant

The discipline of pupils will vary from classroom to classroom. Each teacher makes different demands along disciplinary channels and in the course of a day, a youngster's behavior fluctuates. Every pupil has his own internal time table. On the field this is disregarded, for discipline is absolute and non-changing. Good coaches do not subscribe to the classroom edict that repression develops frustration. Players have a psychological need for more discipline. It makes them emotionally more healthy. Field discipline teaches men to work under pressure and develops confidence. A school can have fifty members of its student body labeled troublemakers, but as long as the remaining pupils exhibit qualities of good citizenship no drastic changes emerge. In football you cannot, must not, have even one errant man, because the spirit of your entire ball club will be corrupted. This type of constant control teaches players to expect the worst of life, otherwise they are living in a fool's paradise. Throughout life one who learns to expect the worst is in a better position to avoid whatever that worst might be.

Drills a Must

The modern classroom teacher has made the drill obsolete. Repeated efforts to develop efficient fundamentals of learning are negligible because the modern educator feels drills without meaning lead to disciplinary problems. Football is different for in training a squad there can be no escape from the tyranny of repetition. Today a coach thinks of players indentured to his drills. Practice is merely repeating everyday the skills needed to win ball games, and they are not based on enjoyment. A team is well disciplined only when habits have mastered the players. Most practice drills carry an unpleasant emotional overtone because they are tied up with hard work.

When it appears to spectators that the coach is democratic enough to allow his quarterbacks to run the team on the game day, that is a delusion. That coach has spent all week conditioning his quarterback by repeating situations he will face in a game until he can run them by rote. It is like throwing darts. The more you throw the greater is the probability of hitting the bull's eye. Every practice of the preceding week is consumed with drills to achieve the coach's objectives.

Good coaching means a drill for every skill and everyone engaged in some drill.

MAINTAINING GOOD DISCIPLINE

The following ten listings will aid in the implementation of good discipline:

1. Winning.
2. Peer acceptance.

3. Converting defiance into praise.
4. Treat your team as men, not boys.
5. Pseudo group decisions.
6. Tension release.
7. Censure must not be personal.
8. The silent treatment.
9. Disciplining your stars first.
10. Face-saving technique.

1. Winning

There is no magic, no bag of tricks, in maintaining effective discipline. There are, however, some factors which are important. It would be folly to list first anything except winning. Winning teams need very little discipline. Winning is a desirable and common aim with which every member of the group is identified. I frankly do not know whether winning leads to good discipline or good discipline leads to winning. What is cause and what is effect? Both elements are important. The fact remains, however, that a team which experiences victory generates its own drive and a minimum of disciplinary problems emerge.

2. Peer Acceptance

Every normal adolescent realizes he must be acceptable to his squad if he is ever to exert much influence upon any individual within that squad. If the team rejects him, it follows no single player can accept him without also incurring the risk of the disapproval by his teammates. Psychologists list this pattern of thought under delusions known as "reference." You, as coach and part of that same group, hold the key. You must strive to make yourself acceptable as a leader of that team. Since you are the recognized leader of this select group, every member automatically will conform to your wishes in order to obtain acceptance by his peers.

A fair, tough, consistent, understanding, and sympathetic coach who learns early this importance of peer acceptance among his squad members lessens the problems of discipline.

3. Converting Defiance Into Praise

During the season there are times that are trying to both the squad and coaching staff. On these occasions the response of some players will tend toward rudeness, contempt, and defiance. Coaches realize this is part of the readying process and feel no personal affront; nevertheless, steps should be taken immediately to block this behavior.

Years ago, one of my tackles loafed on a downfield block. When I pointed it out to him, he turned with a hurt and surprised look which read, "Coach, you are lying. I hustled." The moment I noticed his rudeness and partial defiance, I ordered him to run a lap. He did. We ran a few plays, then I reinserted the erring tackle and instructed the quarterback to run the play where the tackle's assignment took him downfield. There was a marked improvement. I then openly praised the tackle for his hustle. In other words, I created a situation where the tackle's rudeness resulted in his loss of peer acceptance, but converted that into a praise-offering situation. It is merely rebuilding what you take away. As players respond to praise more than fault-finding, you will be wise to sandwich the faults between recognition of portions of their play well done.

I have utilized this type of praise very often. In talking with newspapermen, I mention a specific player and state unequivocally, "This man is going to develop into a star."

I recall bawling out an end for repeating a mistake and later that day having this same man pose for a newspaper picture. The publicity and picture assured the player my criticism was not personal, besides salving the ego I earlier had hurt.

4. Treat Your Team as Men, Not Boys

Treat your squad as young adults, which is flattering to young men. Always address them as men, not boys. A normal adolescent wants ardently to forget his childish past. He longs to be considered as a young man, for this is attractive to the adolescent mind. Referring to them as men makes it easier for the coach to demand adult behavior.

5. Psuedo Group-Decisions

In handling this phase of discipline you must practice group deception. Once you have won the acceptance of your squad you can utilize their love for you to solve problems (see p. 83 on indirect discipline). Players experience a feeling of exaltation when they realize their coach thinks so much of their good judgment that he is asking them to decide. To accomplish this successfully you need a preparatory step. First you summon players to a meeting where you present the issue to the group. It could be a problem in lack of hustle on the part of the backs. You are openly dissatisfied. You tell them you will not have such sloppy and careless playing. Rave about plain generalities for approximately ten minutes. Suddenly you appoint one of your better men to conduct the remainder of the meeting. If you have a captain, appoint him. If you feel your captain is not capable, do not hesitate to bypass him on this occasion. Instruct your appointee, within earshot of everyone else, that you are leaving so they may conduct an open meeting. Instruct them not to leave until it is settled. Ask the man in charge to report to you after the meeting. Never discuss your plans with the man you have placed in charge. His appointment must come as a complete surprise. However, be sure to thank him for his interest and contributions when he reports to you on the results of the meeting. This is the easiest method I know of having a group dominate itself.

I remember the 1951 undefeated team experiencing some difficulty with two prima donnas who were infesting the entire squad with their petty jealousies. Our head coach, Glenn Killinger, sensed there was something wrong among the players. A meeting was called and Little-All-American Tackle Charlie Weber, now with the Chicago Cardinals, was told, "Weber, as captain, your responsibility is to conduct this meeting and not break up until every thing is settled. I will not stand for a few men ruining a fine season. Not at this late stage of the campaign. Thrash out anything that is gnawing at this ball club." A half hour later Weber reported to the coaching staff to inform us, "Everything is going to be all right. Everything is ironed out."

6. Tension Release

During the season boredom sometimes catches up with you and your players. In class you try not to violate the attention span—football is no different. As coach, you must recognize the absurdity of expecting the adolescent player to work at top speed all the time. You must realize that, at times, fluctuations in performances are bound to occur. You also understand that at times, the tension which you have created needs an outlet previous to game participation. As a prudent coach, you must train yourself to accept this fact. You must change gears.

Never Display Your Tensions Before the Squad

When I started to coach in 1935, I was not only guilty of over-coaching but of transferring my anxiety and fears to the players. I would get all wound up and tight as a drum inside. My fear resulted in misplaced aggression. The moment a player fooled around, I jumped him with caustic remarks. I vividly recall practicing in mud before a championship game; Gus Ciffelli, a tackle who later achieved fame with Notre Dame and the Detroit Lions, took a handful of mud and spread it over the face of a guard. I ran him off the field and came close to losing the finest lineman I have ever coached. I was a helluva poor excuse for a coach.

Last year, with one game separating us from an undefeated season, the situation and environment were repeated. It rained and we were working in mud. The tension could have been sliced with a knife. In the midst of a serious practice I took some mud and smeared it all over Bruce Shenk, our Little All American End. Before I knew it, everyone was having a private mud battle to the complete enjoyment of the entire coaching staff. Head Coach Killinger permitted this to go on for five minutes, then said, "Men, we have to go to work now." The mud slinging stopped as swiftly as it began. The men returned to work with renewed zeal.

Another good device we have employed at West Chester when the tension is building is suddenly to stop a play and ask, "Who's afraid of Delaware?" Forty voices respond, "Nobody!" Often Coach Killinger surprises the squad with, "Who's going to lick Delaware?" Our men will yell in unison, "West Chester!" Little do they realize that with each yelling response a huge escape valve opens and a volume of tension is released.

7. Censure Must Not Be Personal

Very often, good coaches interpret the deviate behavior of some players as a personal affront. A player who drinks, smokes, and keeps late hours is not directing his breakage of training rules to the coach, although some coaches interpret his activities as such. There is, nevertheless, a logical explanation for this. Coaching is a personal undertaking to every mentor. It is difficult to react otherwise.

As coach, however, you would be prudent to modify this reaction. In fact, you must condition it. When you personalize an infraction, you then permit your desire for revenge to dictate your coaching. More often than not this will lead to an open conflict and the development of an unpleasant environment. *Eventually you will win, but lose too.* You will conquer the errant player, but your technique will result in loss of squad respect and perhaps the loss of a good player. This type of guerilla warfare will cause whatever good discipline is established to vanish. You must learn to stand above personal vanity. This is a big order, for the path is never smooth and untroubled. Yet it is the only road to earning the respect of your entire ball club.

Three Methods of Handling Rule Breakers

Experience has shown me three methods of handling chronic rule breakers.

1. Call a meeting and discuss the importance of training rules to team success. Drive home your point without mentioning names—look at them long enough so they alone realize you

know. If this fails to produce the needed results, try the next method.

2. Call a private conference where you inform the individual he is suspended from the squad for a week until he mends his ways. Tell him you know he has the guts to return. All champions come back. This action must remain between the two of you. It is not necessary for you as coach to mention this to the squad. Allow him to do that if he chooses. The fact that you make no open mention of his offense will be a factor in his return to your good graces.

3. When the above procedures fail, call an open meeting where no punches are pulled. Be specific with the charges. Name the culprits and command them to turn in their uniforms, never to wear them again as long as you are coach. Once this has been accomplished you abruptly terminate the meeting and dismiss the squad. Anything you may say after that is anti-climactic. It is wise to remember that once you have chosen this bold action you must never relent. Under no condition should you reinstate the fired players.

This technique is most effective in situations where the recalcitrant player is not sensitive and can withstand open criticism.

There exist some important principles underlying this type of action which all coaches should understand.

When disciplining, see that the player directs his dissatisfaction and blind resentment not towards you but towards himself. This makes your reproof and punishment more effective. Attempt to distress the player internally, not only because of his shortcomings but because you as coach have brought it to the conscious awareness of the entire squad. For punishment to be wholesome, two conditions must prevail. First, the player must understand that his punishment is the direct result of his wrongdoing. He created it. Secondly, he must feel that your censure is not personal. You assume he realizes the infliction of punishment is a duty which every coach must carry out—that you still love him as a person.

You hope he understands that you are not doing this in anger or revenge, but in the hope that the punishment will give him the help he needs to regain his former control and status. This type of conduct is not built into the nervous system of either the player or coach. It must be learned.

I remember incidents when players became angry with me because of punitive steps I had taken, I turned to them stating, "Don't get mad at me, I'm on your side. Get mad at your opponents; they are the enemy." This process usually quieted them down.

Last but not least in importance is the folly of referring to disciplinary action once it is past. When you, as coach, pull skeletons from the closet you are guilty of taking unfair advantage of your players. Good coaches bury the incident forever never referring to it again. This is followed with a friendly and warm attitude toward a player who has been punished. By never holding grudges you help a player retain his self respect.

8. The Silent Treatment

Every good coach knows this cunning strategy. It is the silent treatment or pretended unawareness. You merely ignore some player whose performance is sub par. The player overcome with the feeling of mental isolation soon loses status and reforms.

Two years ago I was blessed with a guard whose speed excelled that of any back. His reaction time was excellent. He weighed two hundred lbs. and was six feet tall. He could have played pro ball if he had possessed a different mental attitude. His superior play developed into a deficiency because there was no one else on the squad who could match his skill. As a result he soon became complacent and indifferent. The moment I noticed his self-indispensable appraisal, I had to resort to the "silent cure" to awaken him.

He reported for practice, and I had planned to apply this remedy during a line scrimmage that afternoon. I proceeded to call out the names of the men I wished to start the scrimmage. When I came to his left guard position, I hesitated and looking directly at him I asked, "Where are the left guards?" Immediately four hands went up, including his. I inserted the second string guard. The scrimmage continued for ten minutes and I called plays where the substitute guard would look especially good, and then proceeded to praise the man openly. I added, "Auch, you are going to play a lot of ball come Saturday. You are doing a bangup job."

I then inquired again the identity of the other left guards. Once more I substituted some one else, ignoring the star—then I applied the "ego crusher." I had given everyone except the guard in question the opportunity to engage in the scrimmage. Then I asked, "Is there anyone who has not been in it?" Of course his hand went up and his features assumed a face-saving smile. I looked directly at him then broke up the scrimmage and instructed the line to move upfield for squad work.

The next day I repeated the performance with an added twist. When I called for the left guards I pointed to him and said in complete, convenient ignorance, "What is your name, uh . . . uh." He was further crushed, but repeated his name. I said "Oh! yes," and proceeded to substitute some one else.

The third day of practice I ran him with the third stringers. On the day of the game I failed to start him and played him number three. Following the ball game, which we won, I knew he was cured. Every ensuing practice he was first on the field and hustled as hard as he could. You should, if possible, resort to this during a week when your opponent is a weak one. Not playing this man will hurt you. Try to postpone action until that time unless you find that waiting will hurt you more.

The following statement is extremely important. Coaches should know the threshold of every player. A team is made up of many varied temperaments and you must understand how far a man will allow you to push him before the breaking point is reached.

An example in point was our halfback, Jackie Wendland, who doted on pressure. He loved being kidded, and came to expect it from the coaches. Coach Killinger nourished him on a diet of invectives and taunts. As Wendland weighed only 150 lbs., Killy ridiculed him before the squad by stating "Wendland, Delaware will kill you—they'll hang you on the goal post, you're so little." Wendland answered, "Yeh—look coach, I'm just a little potato but hard to peel. Nobody will hurt me." Of course, Wendland knew when his coach was jesting and when he was really pouring it on. The young man never answered but took his licking when castigated for real. The tone of a coach's voice is the key.

On the other hand, some men go to pieces at the least provocation. Years ago a good guard, named Socia was broken hearted, upset, and wretched because of a scathing remark I made about him. He had had difficulty remembering an assignment, and his missing it repeatedly annoyed me. During a meeting I said "Listen, Mr. El Stupo Socia and I'll chart it for you!" I then proceeded to diagram the play, making the figures 4 feet in size instead of the usual 3 inches. I noticed immediately Socia was dying in that one moment a thousand deaths. The next practice he was a total stranger, not pouting, but suffering from a loss of enthusiasm. He had taken my words to heart. He was hurt.

In Wendland's case his threshold was known, but with Socia I had erred and nearly lost the man. It took a lot of encouragement and kind words to erase the sting of that one remark. Commendation and public acclaim dominated my method of handling him; in fact, that same week a reporter friend did a story on him, quoting me on his virtues. It was my way of evening the score after blundering badly.

9. Disciplining Your Stars First

Every squad has some players whose abilities are admired and respected by their teammates. They are the "stars." Because of the high esteem held for these players, it is necessary that their play and behavior be conducive to effective team control. Stars are imitated, and if they conform the others will follow so much easier. Be constantly alert to see that your stars do not develop into egomaniacs: prima donnas who think they are indispensable and need exert only a partial effort. If you cannot cure them of their self-importance, do not have them around.

A conscientious player was never meant to be a sub for a talented one, but give me plenty of the former, and I will win my share of games. I recall the story of the famous "Four Horsemen" reading their clippings, and what is worse, believing them. Rockne brought them back to earth by starting the second team line during the Purdue game. The "Four Horsemen" were slowed down to a trot. With the insertion of the first team line (Seven Mules) they began to move like real thoroughbreds. Rockne's levelling off trick awakened them to the fact that football is a team effort.

I cured one of my star guards by stating before the entire squad, "Jones, you are just what Coach Smith (a competing coach) said of you—a lemon." The man winced as if cut with a whip. I had no further trouble with him.

Whenever possible, however, make your stars leaders. Talk to your outstanding lineman as if he were the leader and do likewise with an excellent back. This device not only maintains but improves the discipline of your squad.

10. Face-Saving Techniques

Since players are human, they also have need for face-saving techniques. You, as coach, can supply those, and thus maintain good rapport with your squad. An end misses a pass, a back fumbles, a lineman misses a key block—this will happen sometime or another to every player, regardless of stature.

I recall Tommy Donahue, an outstanding end, missing a game winning touchdown pass which would have given La Salle the championship. My heart was broken, but to this day no one ever knew it. I said to Tommy, who wept unashamed, "Tommy, you caught a lot of passes; if you can catch them you are allowed to miss them now and then. One play is only an infinitesimal part of a great many plays which make up a game. You didn't lose this game. In fact, I'm proud of the way you played. You gave it your best, fellow, now get dressed and forget it."

I recall a man whose constant fumbling resulted in our losing two important games. In this case it was pure carelessness. I gave this man a football and ordered him to carry it around all day—

to every class—to and from the lunchroom—and to and from his home. I insisted he do so for a solid week, and I checked to insure that the edict was carried out. He did, and believe it or not, was cured of his excessive fumbling.

On the other hand, I recollect a halfback whose fumble was the deciding factor in a game which we lost. Despite the error, this back gave everything he had every moment. In commenting on the fumble I told him, "I was surprised you didn't lose your teeth along with the ball. I never saw a more vicious tackle, and anyone hit that hard should fumble. I'm giving the defense credit for that one." This illustrates one technique for helping a player regain status in the eyes of his teammates. His devotion and love for you doubles. Young men do not forget those who came to their aid in time of distress.

A more important aspect of coaching which must be understood is the expectancy of error which is prevalent in a player's early career. It takes time to be a finished product, and mistakes will be made, especially in the sophomore year. A wise coach should count his sophomores and figure each will cost him one or more touchdowns during the season. Impatience should give way to understanding.

PREPARING FOR THE OPENING GAME

Many are called but few are chosen

This chapter is designed to explain the relationship prior to and including the opening game. Most high school and college teams repair to a camp site for preliminary training, others remain at home for the early practices. Essentially, however, the relationship which unfolds during this special time is the same and will be treated as such.

Schedule Determines Pre-Season Preparation

No discussion concerned with the relationship involved while preparing for the opener would be complete without some mention of your schedule, especially the opening game. The calibre of your opposition holds the key to your preparation; therefore, this game is important. It not only is a preview of things to come, but determines how strongly and quickly you approach a state of readiness. If you have made the mistake of opening with the toughest team on your schedule, your pre-opener preparation must be pegged to a point where your team must be at mid-season form. They are compelled to play their best football at the very beginning of the season. All other games then become merely anti-climactic.

102

This is a serious breach in the technique of scheduling, yet you read of it being done repeatedly. Why? The reason of course is found in the monetary renumeration which accompanies going out of your class to play an opponent.

Several years ago, West Chester opened its season against a strong Delaware University team. This was by far the best and most formidable team on our schedule. It meant bringing our team to a peak very early in the season, in fact, for our initial game. The desired technique is to bring a team along gradually so it reaches its peak about the middle of the season and maintains that sharp edge throughout. All teams grow better as the season progresses and you should play your best at the time when the most improvement is in evidence. I remember the occasions when we defeated Delaware the victories became the springboard to an undefeated season. On the other hand, when they licked us, it took our team three or four games to recover and level off. It is like putting all your eggs in one basket.

I suggest you avoid any similar situations where your schedule becomes the slave to big monetary returns. To expose young men to competition not commensurate with their own abilities in order to make a few dollars is a most vicious and abominable practice. This action must be discouraged. No opponent should be on your schedule merely because it will make the turnstiles click. Other reasons, such as a common competitive ground, common standards, and a common philosophy toward athletics are more important, and should therefore dictate whom you will play.

Monetary Gains Should Not Be the Master of the Schedule

This scheduling problem can be avoided by meeting with your athletic director and evaluating the situation from all sides. Incidentally, no athletic director should ever schedule an opponent without first consulting his coach. This is a common courtesy. If your athletic director insists that playing a particular school is necessary, in order to provide sufficient funds to purchase equipment, then football should be dropped. Do not become a party to the exploitation of young bodies merely to make money. School football was never intended to make money. It is a sport.

Every time your team takes the field, there should exist at least a 50 per cent possibility of winning. To turn the boys loose against an opponent whom they do not stand a chance to beat is pure folly. The finest football program I know, whether it is in high school or college, is one in which equipment and other expenses are not dependent upon gate receipts. A healthy situation prevails in high school, where the burden of supporting teams rests squarely on the shoulders of the taxpayers. Maintaining athletics should be viewed as any other necessary item in education. Its subsidization should come from the same source as that of books, teachers' salaries, transportation and so forth. It is simply another school expenditure. This makes a sound, healthy climate in high school athletics. It avoids making the equipment of next year's team dependent on this year's successes and failures.

College athletic budgets should operate on a system where the combined proceeds of the student's athletic fees are sufficient to meet the current expenses of all athletic undertakings.

Your Opener—A "Squeeker"

In view of these facts, what type of schedule is a sound one, especially for your opening game? In order for a schedule to qualify as a valid one, it will be necessary to review a team's record five or six years past.

The best opponents are those to whom you lose as often as you defeat them. Playing teams which you vanquish year in and year out is as unjust as playing teams you never beat. It is a wrong turned about and justified on the grounds that you enjoy an advantage and position which, when reversed, is deplorable to you.

It must be understood that athletic directors encounter many problems when attempting to arrange a schedule. Their lot is not an easy one. In fact, many of our larger universities have combined the position of head football coach and athletic director in order to avoid open clashes in personalities because of conflicting philosophies. Every attempt should be made on your part, as coach, to cooperate with your athletic director so that he may better serve you. Patience is essential, for it often requires two or three years to construct a schedule satisfactory to you.

Let us return to the opening game, because it is destined to play a strategic role in your entire season. Should you engage a team you will defeat and get off on the right foot, or should you play a team which will extend you to the limit, chancing a win or defeat in a close one? The latter situation is desired. The first game should be closely contested, regardless of whether the outcome is a victory or a defeat.

A Close Game Has Advantages

A definite advantage will accrue from the closeness of the contest. Winning by a scant margin and barely eking out a victory provides sufficient motivation for a team to work for improvement in its preparation for the next game. A mere reminder of the score of the first game will stir your squad into renewed energy toward gaining increased proficiency through its daily practices.

On the other hand, if you have lost the opener in a closely contested game, an opportunity presents itself whereby you can legitimately drive the squad harder. Their desire to intensify and improve their game in order to win the next one will result in a willing surrender to your practice whip.

The advantage of participating in a game of this sort is that it prevents discouragement among squad members. A victory kindles their desire for more, and a close loss whets their appetites for victory.

Going to Camp

Today most high school and college teams train at a camp. Preparation for camp requires thoroughness. Choosing candidates to make the trip, arranging for lodging, food, practice equipment, and medical supplies is a task of great magnitude.

The best camp is one which accommodates tourists and vacationers, because this site has all the necessary living equipment right there. The fact that your practice will begin at a time when the vacationers are leaving will improve your opportunity of obtaining one of these facilities.

In arranging for your squad to occupy a camp, be certain that you contact a nearby physician to enlist his willingness to treat any illness or injuries during your stay. This is imperative.

Meeting Camp Expenses

Money to defray the expense of a camp can be raised by the varsity club through many varied undertakings. Tickets for big basketball games can be chanced off, candy can be sold at games with the proceeds thrown into a camp fund. Mothers' clubs will be glad to cooperate in two or three annual bake sales. This last venture will help swell the camp treasury. If it is necessary to make up any deficit, then every player should pay a proportionate fee.

Every Candidate Receives a Camp Schedule

Upon departing for camp every man is given a schedule of planned activities. This is a mere extension of football information initiated with your off season correspondence. (See Chapter 10.)

If at all possible arrange to have the squad police itself. Have them establish their own training rules. Of course, you are going to drop seeds of direction in a very subtle manner.

It is important that the squad understand in no mistaken terms the reason for camp. They are there primarily to gain proficiency in football skills. Getting along with their peers, and learning to give and take are bilateral results of this adventure.

Establishing the Temper and Emotional Climate for the Approaching Season

At camp you establish the climate for the season ahead. Strive patiently to improve the skills of the older men and to teach fundamentals to the newer men. Learning fundamentals will not be fun. Build up a mental filing system on each candidate for quick reference when danger signals go up in the future. Learn the threshold of each man, his capacity and liabilities.

You must make your players quality conscious by instilling in them team pride. Inform them that making the team is based upon both quality and quantity of work.

When your men develop the feeling of pride a closeness in team ties results. Pointing out the excellent performances and records of previous ball clubs will aid in developing these attributes.

Be Tough—Perhaps Unreasonable

You should appear tough to some of the men while at camp. For instance, I recall in one of our high school scrimmages one of my backs ran ninety yards, yet failed to score. He was brought down from behind on the two yard line. That evening during our meeting, I made a big production of his failure to go over for a touchdown. I needled him by inquiring if he had stumbled over a blade of grass, stopped for a sandwich, or slowed down to side-step the chalk markers. I looked dead serious and pretended to be earnest. I informed him that any back that runs ninety yards without scoring should be ashamed of himself. Once in the open it is a cardinal sin to be brought down from behind. "Are you going to be one of those triple threat men: Trip, Stumble, and Fall? There is no excuse for it. It is poor judgment in running. I don't want backs who run from goal line to goal line—I want halfbacks who score—who go all the way." I then dismissed the squad.

Naturally, you are happy with such a man, but you have given him something to think about, and the subject is a most valid one. I have discovered in my coaching experience that players improve when they are put under pressure.

Search Your Squad for New Men

As you are constantly losing players, from graduation and for sundry reasons, it is important that you be alert to developing new men while at camp. Keep searching for that candidate who shows evidence of possessing the necessary qualities of developing into a future fine ball player. You will notice raw stuff, but you can mold it. Do not neglect your experienced men in this process by becoming blind to their improvement.

Handling New Men

Do you recall the first day you reported to football camp? No matter how confident you were, the chances are you lost a good deal of it as you reported for the initial workout. Perhaps it did you more good to lose some of that overconfidence, but not to replace it with doubt, uncertainty and fear.

These young men reporting to you for the first time are no different. They are like small boys who whistle as they walk past a cemetery late at night. Young men are young men; they all put their pants on one leg at a time. They are filled with uncertainty. All new candidates have doubts as to their abilities to make good, and they feel somewhat ill at ease in the midst of strange surroundings, strange faces, and unfamiliar situations. You, therefore, must be openly solicitous of their welfare. You have done a good job in orienting a new team member if he:

1. Feels he is part of the squad.
2. Realizes he can make a contribution to the team.
3. Has confidence in school, you, and team members.
4. Understands the system of play.
5. Realizes the importance of hard work and proper attitude as a basis for team success.
6. Has the desire to give of himself regardless of effort required.

Do Not Ignore New Men

One of the most common mistakes committed by coaches when training at camp is to ignore the new men. Nothing discourages a man quicker than being subjected to standing around and being ignored by the coaching staff. It is imperative that individual attention be given every youngster at camp, regardless of his ability.

In 1940 I nearly lost an excellent guard, Jim Gallegher, because I ignored him the first week at camp. This young man knocked on my door one evening and tearfully informed me he was homesick and would like to leave. He was a lost soul in the depths of despair and loneliness. I persuaded him to remain and during the next practice I gave him individual attention, in fact, I ran him with the first team. I then cancelled the evening meeting and instructed two of the experienced men to take him uptown and show him a good time. I gave them movie and spending money from personal funds. This young man developed into an excellent guard, finishing his playing at Villanova University. Today he is an outstanding high school coach in the Hatboro area. I hate to think of what would have happened had he quit the squad on that eventful night. That incident has never been repeated in my coaching career.

To avoid situations of this sort you would be prudent to have your squad participate in some pre-planned amusements.

Camp Amusements

This phase is especially important when coaching high school men. A camp schedule usually runs as follows:

```
7 A.M........Awake....fix beds....arrange room
7:30.........Breakfast
8:30.........Practice
11:30........Shower and prepare for lunch
12 noon....Lunch
1 P.M........Meeting
2 P.M........Practice
5 P.M........Shower and prepare for dinner
6 P.M........Dinner
7 P.M........Meeting
9 P.M........Free time
10 P.M......Bed....lights out
```

This is a complete and confining program which proves most exhausting and annoying to a young squad. It is necessary that this rigorous schedule be punctuated with planned breaks, especially in the evenings. Contact the movie houses in town and ask them to allow you to invite your squad to see a show gratis. The management generally will be more than glad to comply with your wishes. This takes care of two evenings. A third outing could be arranged by visiting some place of importance in the locality. Perhaps seeing a ball game, a carnival or visiting a park.

At West Chester we break up our trying schedule by seeing two movies in a 10-day period and then spending a third evening as guests of the Brandywine Racing Association located in Delaware, five miles from our campus.

We have also divided our squad into two groups, linemen and backs, and play an intra squad softball game. The losers are required to do all the cleaning chores for the next three days. The winners, besides being relieved of camp work, receive an extra dessert at dinner.

Open House

In my experience some of the finest friends you have can also become some of your worst enemies—parents. In order not to have parents straggling in and out of camp breaking up the training routine, you should plan an open house. By following this procedure you are limiting parental visitations to one day. This becomes an important and gigantic task in social engineering. Essentially, these duties are chiefly yours.

During one of the evening meetings, supply each man with stationary and instruct him to write his parents inviting them to the camp's open house. Have him inform his parents that an intra-squad scrimmage will be played in the afternoon, and that they are also invited to have dinner with the squad that evening. Collect the letters and mail them for the squad. I suggest you write special invitations to school officials and to anyone who was active in raising money for the camp. Do not forget these folks. Spare no pains to insure the comfort of each parent.

You would be prudent to cancel the afternoon meeting in order that parents will have an opportunity to "hob nob" with their sons.

Be sure every man participates in the game long enough to permit parents to concur in your evaluation of their particular son at the planned evening meeting.

After dinner hold your usual meeting inviting parents to attend. You then proceed to comment on the scrimmage, taking time to evaluate each player. Be wise and include a smattering of praise with the liabilities of each man. Assure the young men with a deficiency that it takes time to develop the fundamental skills, and with a little more practice and maturity they will come. The fact that parents have had visual evidence of the facts you point out will go a long way in cementing coach–parent relationship.

Thank every parent for his cooperation, and stress how much you appreciate their permitting their sons to participate and share in the football camp experience.

Cutting the Squad

Coaching evidently was not designed for mental comfort. A lack of mental comfort is always accompanied by physical discomfort. The mere thought of cutting the squad is grim. This is one of the most distasteful tasks confronting a mentor. It is even more upsetting than losing to a traditional opponent. It is a venture heavily laden with emotional overtones, yet it cannot be by-passed.

You will find that there are three types of players comprising your squad:

1. Those willing and able.
2. Those able and not willing.
3. Those willing and not able.

The first type will be your bread and butter men. Upon their contributions will rest your success.

The second group you get rid of immediately. They will win games for you, but in the long run they will lose more than they win. Utilizing this calibre of player will cause you sleepless nights, for they never play up to their fullest capacities. You will hate yourself for even tolerating this group. It is better to suffer the humiliation of an honest loss than to have this sort humble you with their lack of effort. No good can ever come to you with this class of player.

It is the third category which will tug at your heart strings, because they are willing but not able. God just did not gift these men with sufficient raw material to do the job. Yet they go at it every day, unaware of their natural limitations. They never want for effort.

In my coaching career these men tried so hard that I found it difficult to cut them; in fact, some I retained worked so diligently that they developed into hand-made mechanical men who did a partially good job. However you must gird yourself for the unpleasantness of the task and cut some. Be certain in your meetings that all coaches agree on the feasibility of cutting a man. If there is the slightest doubt in the mind of any member of the staff then keep the player. No one should leave football thinking he has received a fast shuffle. Once a season starts, never cut a man because he lacks ability. Sink or swim with your early decision.

Whenever I have cut a man from the squad, I have always felt that there were two failures involved. First, there was the failure of the man to make good; second, my failure as a coach to develop him into a successful player.

Techniques Employed When Cutting a Man

This task should be done in private. However, you can establish an emotional tone for it by discussing the inevitable during one of your evening meetings. Mention in passing the need to reduce the number of the squad. Inform the team that only eleven men can play at any one given time, and only a select few can be substitutes. Tell them soon some will be cut but never to stop trying; that the word "American" ends in, "I CAN," "A winner never quits and a quitter never wins." Repeat often how much you appreciate their efforts despite their shortcomings. I had a little college end who weighed 135 pounds. His heart was bigger than his entire body but his lack of size and weight would not permit me to play him. Today he is one of our better trainers.

When the day of doom arrives, summon the men to be cut into your office individually and unknown to each other. This requires a lot of courage. Some coaches still utilize the cold, impersonal method of posting the names of the men retained, saying nothing to the cut ones. Please do not utilize that plan.

Talk face-to-face to the man to be cut. Open your talk in a friendly manner, but be sure your approach suits the individual. Be frank and firm with the man about his shortcomings. You must explain to the man where he has fallen down. It seems easier to evade the issue, but sooner or later it will catch up with you. You merely are postponing the inevitable.

Sometimes you will want to come to the point immediately, especially in dealing with players who know how to take the shock. Many times, however, you will find it desirable to point out both the good and bad characteristics of the player—leading into his shortcomings gradually. Checking with him each of his weaknesses point by point enables you to accomplish your purpose without sounding artificial and insincere.

Avoid generalities in favor of specific illustration of what you mean. Be sure he recognizes his deficiency. If you think this man can soon overcome his faults tell him specifically how that can be accomplished. This man is not cut outright. You are merely cutting him from the varsity squad and reassigning him to the jay-vee team. The jay-vee coach will be informed of his deficiency and will be instructed how to overcome the player's limitation. Before the player leaves, divulge the plan of action which you have suggested to the jay-vee coach to help make him into a finished product.

Once this man has joined the jay-vee squad and has overcome his weakness, bring him back up to the varsity. This system cushions the blow and holds out a ray of hope for all members of that lesser team.

Several years ago I had a guard at West Chester who had difficulty pulling out of the line to block ends. As this is one of our bread and butter offensive maneuvers, it simply had to be mastered. During practice I repeatedly pointed out how his slowness in pulling out was delaying the play to the point that it was no longer efficient. He understood. Together we suggested a plan for improvement. He spent half of the season with the jay-vee squad. Quite often I would walk over after our practice to observe him and offer encouragement. When I noticed a marked improvement I brought him up to the varsity squad, where he remained until his graduation.

Handling this type of problem is only half as difficult as the one which follows. In this instance you must cope with the man who has such limited ability that he can never make your squad. Remember you always look at a football player and judge him not where he is today, but where he will be in another season or two. You have done that, and in this case you cannot see that additional training will result in acquiring the necessary playing skills. In other words, you must cut this man outright. Once again you have a heart-to-heart talk and explain to the man that he lacks certain abilities. Thank him for his loyalty and cooperation. Wish him luck and Godspeed in his undertakings. Promise never to lose touch with him, despite his lack of football ability.

Make Some Managers and Trainers

Football does not consist solely of players and coaches. Managers and trainers occupy just as important a role as a good lineman or back. Whenever possible, try to direct some of the men you cut into the fields of manager, trainer, statistician or personal aide to you. These new responsibilities will take care of assigning at least eight of the men you are compelled to cut. It helps these men save face and eases their disappointments. They are still associated with the game, but in a different capacity. One of our finest managers at West Chester, Fred Thompson, was at one time a guard candidate. He adjusted to his new assignment and proved just as happy as if he were playing.

Handling the Willing and Able

While at camp this group must be kept insecure up until four days before the opening game. Since you already know what they can do, it is wise to experiment with the new men. Going to camp gives you approximately fifteen practice days before the first game. This is ample time to give a thorough trial to every man on your squad. Play your veterans just enough so that they do not lose confidence. Keep them constantly feeling uncertain and afraid that some new man is going to beat them out for their position.

A good coach soon learns what a player can do best. In intra-squad scrimmages, you can give a veteran a real scare by calling special plays wherein the new man excells. Then openly praise the play of the neophyte. Of course, there will be much that a novice cannot accomplish successfully—work hard on those aspects of his game, but for special purposes show off his finer points. The time will soon come when the rookie will develop proficiency and become a veteran too. Then you merely use another green man and repeat the process.

It is a vicious cycle with the men never catching on to your cunning scheme.

Four days before the opening game, however, it is mandatory that you work your team as a unit. A varsity should be chosen along with a second unit, and game readiness now includes stability of your chosen groups.

Handling Team Injuries

How injuries will be handled must be established the first day of your camp practice and carried throughout the season. A pre-arranged routine should be clear for everyone to follow. A good rule is to insist that every man report any injury to one of the coaches, who in turn notifies the head coach. For pulls, sprains and bruises, have the man go to the doctor's office. A better plan is to arrange with your team physician to see the men at a specified time. Most doctors with whom I have worked prefer an early morning hour or late evening hour. Nine in the morning or nine in the evening are the most desired. You then do not interfere with the medical man's private practice.

The important phase to remember is that every member of your squad feels that the medical treatment afforded him is the best, and the means of obtaining it is simple.

When a man is injured and requires hospitalization, see to it that you visit him every day and instruct the members of the squad to do likewise. Flowers, reading material, "goodies," and get-well cards should be sent in abundance. If the man is confined to his home, visit him just as often.

I have seen too many coaches win a game and go off to celebrate with their cronies, leaving the injured to the attention of an assistant coach. You cannot and must not relieve yourself of that responsibility. A coach who neglects this phase of player relationship at a time of injury does not deserve the privilege of handling young men.

Replacing Injured Men

Very few teams complete a season without being wracked with injuries to key men. In my early coaching career I fretted so much over the loss of a good man that my fears were transferred to the entire team. I watched them lose heart and confidence, and reflect my own attitude that the chances of winning were considerably reduced. Today I do not worry about our team's loss because of an injury. Worry cannot help you. Psychologists tell us worry is the emotion of the evader. Here the evasion is not wanting to play the game without the injured man. Whenever an injury incapacitates one of our men, I immediately turn all my energies toward getting a replacement ready. More excellent football players were developed because of our urgent necessity for a substitute than I can ever begin to enumerate.

Go about the task of readying an alternate with the air and confidence that the man in question will be equal to the occasion. In due time your optimism will infect the entire squad.

chapter seven

ROARS AND SCORES

your relationship with a winning squad

Treat people nicely on the way up, because you are liable to meet them on the way down——ANON

A special relationship comes to the surface when coaches and players are enjoying the roars and scores that mark a successful season.

Blueprint for Victory

Chapter four listed four necessary ingredients for the development of good sound football, but no formula for winning can be complete without adding two more important components. They are:

1. Conditioning
2. Morale

Conditioning

Every winning team is a well geared, conditioned squad. At West Chester, we win a great number of games on the strength of our conditioning process. Our men are just as fresh at the end of a game as the beginning. This fitness is realized by pushing players beyond their threshold of fatigue. Compel them to go a little more when exhausted. This "plus" reduces fatigue to a minimum.

Morale

Morale alludes to obeying the rules of the game whether coaches are satisfied with their intent or not. A byproduct of good morale is a feeling of oneness. All for one and one for all.

To achieve this brand of morale, many factors must be taken into consideration. First is the belief that football morale cannot be limited to just the players and coaches. This is an element which involves the cooperation of the entire school. The administration and the faculty cannot be divorced from participation in the development of this essential.

In this modern world, owing to the increased complexity of society, life is being dominated more and more by the material aspects of social life. This has produced a strain of inconsistency in the code of social conduct. Athletics, especially football, is a victim of this strain and conflict. Proof of this condition is found in the various techniques some coaches use in attempting to beat the rules. Every year the rule makers plunge into the task of making the laws more stringent and foolproof. The great utilitarian philosopher, John Stuart Mill, once wrote, "Men are men before they are teachers, lawyers, or doctors. . . . If you make them honest and capable men, they will make themselves honest and capable teachers, lawyers, and doctors."

This applies to players. If all the forces which play a part in shaping a young man's life stress honesty and integrity, it is bound to rub off in athletics. Honesty in the classroom, in the home, on the playground, make for consistency. There cannot be two codes.

As a coach, you must never permit a breakage of the rules regardless of the resulting advantage. By insisting on this principle, you will encourage good morale.

Coaching is tantamount to the direction of an assembly line. You first perfect the ingredients—the parts. Once this has been accomplished, merely put them together.

As the majority of these ingredients are common and deal

mainly with the mechanics of the game, nothing further will be written about them. The author will concentrate on the relationship which evolves from week to week following a win or previous to a victory.

ORIENTATION FOR WINNING

All good coaches instill in their players a burning desire to win. The will to excell, to be the best, must be drilled into the very lives of each squad member with the fanatical zeal of a missionary. The only reward forthcoming to players is winning. Regardless of what we read and hear to the contrary there is nothing intrinsically wrong with wanting to win. Playing the game just for fun is pure jargon. It is equal to doing a full day's work, not for pay but for the mere fun of it.

American athletes dote on competition, for it becomes a springboard to success. Reasons to the contrary are doubletalk. People who live in glass houses should not take baths in the daytime.

Because there is no other way—except winning—the following pages will present definite reasons to strengthen a coach's winning philosophy.

The fact that all competitive sports list winning ingredients is sufficient evidence that there is not now, and never has been, an acceptable substitute for winning. People who preach "lose with grace" are rationalizing their inability to win. What else is left when you lose except to bow nobly? It reminds me of the White House Easter Egg Hunt. The White House attendants place the eggs about the lawn in full view of the entire White House group. To have those people express surprise at what the kids have found is most amusing. Did they not place them so they could be discovered? Why the surprise?

If a team's purpose is not to win then it leaves only one other alternative—losing. How could losing ever be realized without someone winning? I hope the reader is absorbing the fallacy of the new philosophy.

Why has not some great athletic figure invented a system where both teams lose? Obviously the answer will be the same reason why someone failed to contrive a scheme whereby both teams win.

Where can a young athlete wishing to prepare himself for a losing athletic career purchase a book on *How to Excel in Losing* or *The Technique and Art of Losing?* Winning is an important phase of American life. Losing is only a byproduct of winning— never an objective. If losing is such an accomplishment and such an honorable undertaking, why didn't we send our losers to the Olympic games? Why isn't losing a carry over into adult life instead of success?

There is no adulation or hero worship for losers; that is reserved only for winners.

To the Victor Belong the Spoils

To further solidify a coach's position that there is no alternative to winning, I offer the following proof:

Today, prominent athletes are induced to sign testimonials for all types of products from "Wheaties" to garters. Two box tops become a magic medium of exchange for pictures of sporting heroes.

Young audiences throughout America have been sold products because they were associated with champions.

Growing children identify themselves with athletes who have met the challenge of competition, and retained or won new laurels. It is through this association that youngsters learn the value of wanting to excel—of wanting to be the best.

Turnstiles Do Not Turn

If pennants and championships were awarded to losing teams, the public would clamor to see them play. Experience tells us that losing teams lose more than what scores indicate—they lose money. The public simply refuses to back a team which is mired deep in defeats.

American football is so thrillingly attractive to spectators that they buy season tickets months in advance; drive as many as 600 miles round trip in one day to see a winning ball club. These same people then discuss the victory all year round. No other activity in America, not even the inauguration of a new President draws spectators from coast-to-coast, as does the Army-Navy Game. Without the anticipation of victory by partisans of both teams these long trips would never materialize. As long as they feel their team could win they will attend. The moment the hope of victory fades, attendance drops.

The Changing Role of the Church

Today church leaders have developed a new appreciation of the importance of physical well being. Churches of practically all denominations have given attention to their role as a social institution by turning to the medium of athletics. A hundred years ago, churches were built on hillsides surrounded by cemeteries; today they are built adjacent to playgrounds and tennis courts. Every church basement has a basketball court. Instead of preparing man for death, the new religious philosophy seeks to prepare men for life.

The numerous church basketball and baseball leagues throughout the country attest to this fact. The important fact here is that winning in a church league is equally as important as winning in the big leagues. If you are an observant spectator at the next sporting event take a moment to count the clergy in attendance. The number will surprise you.

Is Winning Malignant?

In recent years, educators and the press have detected a malignancy in American athletics which they have attributed to an increased emphasis upon winning. This they considered a threat to a solid sporting structure. To deny the existence of this conscious growth is pure folly. Investigations within the last ten years have verified the presence of evil threads in the pattern of our athletic fabric. Remedial measures are necessary to eradicate this disease. Steps have already been taken and new ones are forthcoming. Changes in the Ivy League's philosophy and aid to athletes in the Big Ten are recent examples. Because of the sensational exposé of bribery and gambling, some modern educators have proposed the abolition or curtailment of some athletic programs. We hear no suggestion that marriage be abolished because husbands and wives are unfaithful and the divorce rate is high. No one has recommended that manufacturers cease making automobiles because thousands of Americans are killed yearly in traffic accidents.

Every coach worth his salt should strive to keep his program a healthy one.

WORLD UNITY PROMOTED

The many reasons cited previously may be augmented by the national and international prestige which also results from winning.

National Unity Through Sports

National unity is promoted through athletics. The Rose, Cotton and Sugar Bowls when examined have a cultural viewpoint —an instrument for the promotion of togetherness. New Year's day finds the entire country concentrating on various T.V. channels viewing their favorite teams. Seventy million people see these contests and urge their team to victory. Every pair of eyes is looking for that particular play which will spell victory. The prestige which accrues to the winning team far exceeds that experienced by the loser.

Citizenship cannot be made solely through math and science but by an increased sharing in the responsibilities and privilege of every day life. Citizenship results from the realization that one's destiny is bound to the destiny of the group. Any educational means which tends to engender and strengthen this feeling of group solidarity, even if it be athletics, amply justifies its existence as a fundamental part of American education.

International Unity Through the Olympics

It has been made clear to us that peace and international understanding no longer can rest upon a foundation built along economic interests alone. At least it has not up to this writing. Something else is needed. The missing denominator could be play. Athletics on an international scale similar to the Olympics but repeated four times a year could be a cure for this ailing world. To have nations achieve superiority in the sporting world could supply the prestige which previously was fulfilled through war. Winning on the battlefield would give way to winning in the arena.

WINNING DEPENDS ON ANTICIPATORY PLANNING

Synoptic Vision

As a football coach interested in winning the respect and confidence of your players, planning looms up as very important. You become an architect at work. Never plan for one game, as it is an isolated activity. Planning is done for the entire season even though it is still the month of August. This can be accomplished only through synoptic vision, for that enables you to predict fairly successfully the strength and weaknesses of all your opponents. In late August you live in advance, mentally and emotionally, the experiences which your schedule will produce. If you expect success as a coach you must anticipate and must possess imagination.

In 1951 Leo Durocher executed synoptic vision, imagination and courage in manipulating the New York Giants. Some writers called it luck. It amuses me to read that all winning coaches are called lucky. Luck could be defined as thorough planning. In the spring of 1951 Durocher made four fundamental switches in the nine positions. Thompson moved from center field to third base, Whitey Lockman from left field to first base, and Monty Irvin from first to left field. These moves were topped with an untried kid named Willie Mays, assigned to play center field. This team went on to win the pennant. These plans were in his mind, then on paper and finally implemented in the pre-season training.

Last year's undefeated West Chester team was made possible through the imagination of head coach Glenn Killinger. We anticipated a weakness at end. He suggested converting a guard, then a fullback to center and finally a fullback to left half. Each man proved to be effective in his new position.

Approved Espionage

Synoptic vision and pre-season planning would never be successful without an approved system of espionage. In coaching terminology this means keeping charts on your opponent's personnel. Good coaches know as much about the strength and weaknesses of every man on every team on their schedule as they do about their own players. It is impossible to plan a complete season if you are aware only of your own squad's liabilities and assets. Planning would be cloudy and nebulous. You must build your strength to exploit others' weaknesses. As a result, coaches keep up to date files and charts on their opponents' personnel. A knowledge of your deficiencies and potentials, plus those of your opponents, culminates in successful planning.

WINNING ATTITUDE

Attitude is a basic ingredient of every winning team. Two distinctly emerge which need description.

1. Player attitude.
2. Coaching attitude.

1. Player Attitude

Proper player attitude is a must, if a coach expects to have a successful season. The attitudes toward each other, toward the coaching staff, and toward work are most important. It has been my experience that no one can participate in a game as violent as football without the proper frame of mind. Winning teams perpetuate worthy attitudes; the problem stems from establishing winning habits.

Willingness to practice every day to perfect game skills is a manifestation of good player attitude. The minute football players refuse to punish themselves daily to reach and remain in top condition, your season is doomed. I don't want men to play who look at football as just a chore or a job. I want my men to play for the sheer joy of licking someone.

I fired a tackle years ago because I heard him say during a gruesome, fatiguing practice, "Five more minutes and we're in, fellows." I ran him off the field immediately with the remark, "Jones, you can't play for me—get out of here forever and get a job as a time keeper." To him practice was something to endure until he could give attention to personal plans of a more pleasurable nature. He just did not possess the attitude we require.

My men must be overcome with a burning desire to compete, for that is a necessary adjunct to willingness to practice. The tactical refinement of your game plan is fine, but it doesn't mean a thing if your men are not blocking, tackling, and knocking somebody down. They should run into their opponents as though they enjoy it, because they have the desire.

Pride must be mentioned as a significant element in attitude. Players must take pride in their play. They must hurt when they lose. Any player who loses and is satisfied could never play for me. I want men on my squad who take the blame for a defeat and refuse to accept any other reason for failing. I want a hole to burn in them until accounts are squared. No mental rest can ever be felt by a real contestant who has suffered defeat. Words will not salve them, irrespective of the source. I want my men to suffer mental anguish when they are outscored. Pride will cause all of these symptoms to gnaw at their inners and a better effort will follow.

Watch your men walk in after a loss. If they refuse to place their arms around their sweethearts, if they ignore their parents and want no comfort, if they have difficulty eating or sitting still —then you have real competitors. Playing winning football must be similar to a passion which consumes the entire body. Anything short of this is athletic rationalization.

In 1957 our next-to-last game was against Bloomsburg, a team we should have licked by fifty points. As the game unfolded we were lucky to win; in fact, Bloomsburg won in everything but the score. We should have paid to get in. We had no line charge. They were just standing there pawing around, shaking hands with the other linemen. We lacked speed and precision as a team. We had taken too much for granted—the players and coaches too had forgotten about paying the price in practice.

The following week we had to defeat California Teachers to

realize an undefeated season. It was a romp, and we won 62-0. What made it an easy ball game was the dignity that every player felt—pride that was ruffled in their poor exhibition the week before. They were so flushed with confidence in their ability, that as a team they felt a compulsion to lather some one—and did.

I once heard Glenn Killinger address his players at a football meeting, telling them in a definite, incontestable tone of voice, "I will not stand for a losing team." Of course, I am a disciple of his, and second that philosophy. I once overheard George "Lefty" Demko, one of our captains say, "At West Chester, we're afraid to lose."

2. Coaching Attitude

As a coach, you must have confidence. It borders on arrogance and conceit, but it is not. It is a feeling of self-reliance, a certainty. It is not quite cocksureness nor boldness, but a faith in yourself and your team. It must never be obnoxious. You must not appear conceited—only honest. You, as a coach, have the desirable attitude when you assume that a play failed, not because the opponent was superior, but because some one failed to carry out his assignment. It is this basic attitude that enables you constantly to push your men into a superior effort. Once you are convinced that your men can lick anyone, then day after day, hour after hour, you can drill them into errorless performances. Football is a game of mistakes, and winning teams make the fewest. Your intent is to develop the fastest, sleekest, most precise team in the world. This you accomplish through hard work. You repeat day in and day out the drills which perfect game skills—and then hope your errors are reduced to a meaningless few.

Good coaching attitude is in evidence when you look upon each opponent on your schedule as the best. I was asked once, "Who is the toughest team you play?" I answered, "Whatever club we are playing this Saturday." Every week we prepare to play our toughest opponent regardless of who it is. We treat every opponent the same. We do not have any big game as so many other teams do. Our big game is the next game. Regardless

of who it may be, we strive to get a riled-up ball club. It is necessary to take one game at a time. Every Saturday is a separate
war all its own. Certainly good coaches engage in advance planning but never so it detracts from the contest at hand. Players
and coaches alike must share the philosophy that any time eleven
men are pitted against eleven others, any score may result. No
team ever won a football game because of favorable press clippings, or on its past record. A team must be sharp—the men
must block and tackle every Saturday in order to insure success.

Coaching Dissatisfaction a Must

The successful outcome of every football game is determined
by making fewer mistakes than your opponent. As a result, you,
as coach, conduct a constant vigil to spot flaws and correct them.
It is a never-ending crusade for every other coach stresses iden-
tical principles and philosophies.

When your club loses, you correct blunders, because the score
has proven you made more than the other team. It is when you
win that players find it difficult to understand why their coach is
unhappy. Good coaches are pleased but never make their players
aware of their contentment.

After every victory a coach finds fault. The following week he
dwells on the errors, giving only perfunctory attention to the
excellent performances of individuals. The outstanding play of
some individuals is mentioned to the entire squad but the lapses
committed are treated like mortal sins. There are two reasons for
this. First, it is a coaching point that impresses the entire squad
that a deficiency exists and you will not condone it. Secondly, it
brings the squad back to earth, and convinces them that their
victory was not as glorious as they at first believed.

If it were not for a consistent dissatisfaction on the part of a
mentor, players would soon assume they are good and no longer
need coaching nor extensive practice.

As a coach you must be convinced that every performance
could have been a better one.

Last year, our West Chester team protected their undefeated
skein with a magnificent goal line stand to halt Bloomsburg only

one yard from pay dirt. It was heart-warming to their line coach
to see them rise to the occasion and repel four solid thrusts at
their goal line. It was the most outstanding feat of the entire ball
game, and the linemen felt smug about their tenacity. The following Monday I raised hell with that gallant line. They were
crushed that I would find fault with them, but soon agreed when
I said, "If you had been playing ball all afternoon they would
never have reached your goal line, and the stand would have
been unnecessary. In fact, that goal line stand proved you were
loafing for if you could stop them down there, you could have
stopped them elsewhere. I don't want men who play only ten
minutes out of every fifteen." They couldn't win for losing. Of
course, you are pleased as punch and do not believe what you
have said to them, but it does establish the mood and emotional
tone of the practice week ahead.

The following statements have tremendous impact and importance for every coach. Remember, if you are satisfied with the
play of your charges you will become complacent and will stop
coaching. That is the time when you and your team will be in
for a real clobbering; therefore, never be happy with their performances. Find fault even if you have to stretch reality and
truth to do it. When you cease to find fault, winning is in
jeopardy.

Last season, Head Coach Killinger was ill and missed the entire week of practice and failed to make the Baldwin-Wallace
trip. In our 12 years of working together he had never missed
a game. As the team was undefeated and we felt they could go all
the way, a heavy responsibility rested upon my shoulders. To
write that I felt equal to the task is not conceit, but honesty, for
the old master had trained me to run a ball club exactly as he
would. I asked the squad to play their hearts out for their head
coach, who was absent only in the flesh, for in spirit he was on
the sideline looking over their shoulders. The men hit the field,
and before the quarter was up they were leading 21-0. As the
game progressed, the lead was increased to 35-0. Baldwin-
Wallace was able to muster a real march which culminated in a
score on the old end-around play. It was beautifully executed,

but gave me cause for alarm. After the game I congratulated them, saying nothing about the opponent's score. It was written earlier that good coaches never mention mistakes in the dressing room immediately after a contest. Returning from Ohio they were a proud, pleased and haughty group. It was a noisy, merry-making squad intoxicated with triumph that rode the bus back to West Chester. I permitted them to enjoy every moment of it —but—when the men reported for Monday's practice a short and terrifyingly rapid change had taken place. I was furious, and vented my rage on the defensive linemen for permitting a team to score against an 8-3 defense with an end-around play. As Baldwin-Wallace's left end had scored, I took a position behind our own left end and measured off seven big yards. With each step I said, "How could an end start here, run past the center, the left tackle, the left guard, the right guard, the right tackle, the fullback, the right end and score standing up? I don't know. You tell me. Go ahead! One of you eight men, up front, please tell me how it could be done?"

That scene was something they had not reckoned with and they settled down to the work at hand. It was a quick technique intended to bring them back to earth. Never stop finding fault, regardless of how superlatively they execute their assignments.

At the end of the season however, this strategy ceases and you just cannot heap enough praise on them.

WINNING OVER A WEAK OPPONENT

Complacency—a Disease

Consecutive victories usually provide a breeding ground for a common bacteria known as "complacency." Every coach must exercise extreme caution to prevent such a disrupting disease. This affliction strikes coaches as well as players and results in a loss of team proficiency. Losing provides its own thrust, winning diminishes the drive. It is natural for players who execute their tasks successfully day in and day out to feel self-satisfied. This mental attitude coupled with the fact that they can read about their opponent's losses removes incentive to practice hard in order to reach razor sharpness. Whatever a coach tells them about the possibility of defeat by a weak team loses its impact on the players if they believe press reports, in spite of warnings to the contrary.

In readying for an adversary whose record is not impressive, you must stress fundamentals. This indulgence will never hurt your squad.

Overcoming Complacency

There are two methods of overcoming complacency. One is playing someone else and the second is applying the needle to rekindle the spark of ambition. As coach you should never hesitate to insert someone else in place of any man afflicted with complacency. Granted, the substitute has inferior ability, but that equals out when the varsity performer is not playing up to his full potential.

Another way to bring a complacent player back into line is to expose him to ridicule. A few words can be surprisingly effective if they attack his ego, for this is the region where he is most vulnerable. Two personal experiences best illustrate this:

Last year one of our outstanding linemen was being given Little All-American consideration. His play was superlative; however, we noticed a smug satisfaction overcoming this young man. Evidently he was beginning to believe his press clippings. For approximately a week I was looking for an excuse, an opening to embarrass him into coming back to reality. The opportunity finally unfolded. I overheard him feuding with our equipment man for a new pair of socks. This was the second consecutive day he had made a similar request. He became adamant in his insistence.

I walked out to the men's dressing quarter, feigning the need for a drink of water. Returning, I said to our equipment man, within everyone's hearing, "Al, give this man a pair of socks. Don't you know who he is? Why, he is Mr. Smith, the great Little All-American lineman. What's wrong with you, Al—don't you read the papers? This man's good and should be accorded preferential treatment. Haven't you read how Smith and ten other guys have won all those games for us?" I returned to complete my dressing, saying nothing more. During practice I went on as if the incident had never taken place. Smith's attitude had changed, and with that, his play regained its efficiency.

Another incident took place during my tenure at LaSalle. I had an outstanding tackle whose size alone had destined him for athletic prominence. Possessing a body 6'4" tall and weighing 230 lbs. simplified his desire to lord over everyone else.

Confidence is like electricity. It can do immense good or immense harm. In this instance, it was harnessed to the egocentricity of a young man convinced he no longer needed practice, let alone coaching. I sawed wood until the opportune moment. It presented itself in the midst of one of my practice scrimmages. Because Smith, the tackle, was loafing, a second-string end put a real block on him. He was so surprised and embarrassed that he punched the little end and broke his nose. My anger could not be contained. As the trainer ran out to administer to the hurt man I moved under Smith's nose and said furiously, "You are a self-satisfied, opinionated jackass who is bigger than the team— the coach—the school, all put together. Now get out of here. Go take a look at yourself and come back when you see what I do."

I found him waiting at the dressing room door, apologizing sincerely to the end and to the entire squad and coaching staff. A partial satisfaction resulted from that incident, for a real friendship developed between these two men which culminated in their opening a law firm together.

Timeconomy

This is the opportune time to give your men some new plays to be used two or three games hence. The advantage of perfecting new techniques now is found in the time element. Football mentors call this "timeconomy," for an essential saving of time results which will be more in evidence in a month or so.

It is prudent to allow your men to assume the new variations will be used in the coming contest. This prevents any depreciation in enthusiasm. Simply be careful to instruct your quarter-back in the dressing room just prior to game time not to use the new plays until you send word in. You have other plans for them in the weeks ahead, but the players must not be aware of your scheme.

Often a Negative Result

When you play a poor team and defeat them rather handily, your ball club may not look good, regardless of the score. You may overwhelm a team 48-0 and still appear only a fairly pre-cisioned team. The calibre of the opposition is one of the decid-ing factors in how well you appear to be playing. Experience will tell you that a negative result can accrue. Your men may not look sharp. This should not worry you, for as coach, you are confronted with a healthy situation. Healthy because you have won, but neither you nor your men are satisfied with their per-formances. This relieves you of the whip to drive them in preparing for next week's game.

Don't Lay It on

In this game of football there is no assurance that you will always head a winning aggregation. There will come a time when you will be on the losing side of the field, dying a thousand deaths. Despite the fact that coaches compete for supremacy, there does exist a kinship which they share. This brotherhood manifests itself when you are in the driver's seat. Don't lay it on. The old saying is that if you lead by less than three touchdowns, it is not enough, and if you lead by more than four, you are rubbing it in.

Good coaches know instinctively when a game is wrapped up and send their subs in for the necessary experience.

In 1953 Youngstown University was leading West Chester 35-0 at halftime. Dike Bede, the Youngstown coach, played his second and third teams the entire second half to save us from further embarrassment. We appreciated his kindness, for he could have scored a hundred. The game ended 35-6.

It is an understanding coach who will meet his adversary in the center of the field after the game and apologize if the score is overwhelming. It is also a nice gesture to distinguish some outstanding player on the vanquished team and sing his praises to the defeated coach.

Competition is contagious but so is cooperation. When you give a fellow coach a break, you make things easier for yourself. If an opposing coach no longer feels you are a threat to him, he stops being a threat to you.

The biggest tragedy in football is that one of the coaches must lose. A covert commandment is to glory or die inside, but outwardly gentlemanly qualities must be evident.

WINNING OVER A GOOD TEAM

Realizing a victory over a good team requires confidence and a winning attitude. This must be established through the coach's relationship with the team throughout the entire year and emphasized the week preceding the big game. It can never be developed overnight, like mushroom growth. Players should share an innermost belief in the coach's aptitude to solve the problem areas presented in meeting this formidable opponent. It is a faith of unsuspecting certainty which they hold in your talent as coach to improvise some new scheme destined to culminate in the defeat of this squad whose ability is equal to your own.

Bobby Dodd, the great Georgia Tech coach, once stated, "To defeat a ball club which is on a par with your own team requires resorting to special stratagem. You must:

1. Fool them.
2. Outmaneuver them.
3. Surprise them.

1. Fooling Them

The only feasible method of fooling an opponent is to withhold some phase of your play until you face them. The only time you deceive a team is when you have developed proficiency in some aspect of the game which heretofore was missing. Coaches with defensive plans against you will give only passing attention to apparent weaknesses in your repertory of plays. As a competent coach, you must see your teams as opposing mentors see them. Once you have cultivated that ability, you notice your own deficiencies and establish a remedial and improvement program. By the time you play this team your defects have not only been overcome but they have been converted into your strongest assets. Therein lies your ability to fool your rival, for you are now successfully executing play patterns which previously were liabilities. Plays that were total losses in gaining yardage suddenly become your best gainers.

Last year we were victims of this. In scouting Bloomsburg it was evident that they had no outside strength. Our practice sessions failed to include plans to stop their end runs. The day of the game they ran our ends as if they owned them. We were fooled because some skills were withheld during their previous games with the intent of saving them for West Chester. Coach Blair of Bloomsburg evidently made judicious use of "timeconomy."

2. Outmaneuvering Them

Football today has become a game of tactics. All coaches strive to enjoy a tactical advantage over their opponents. It has developed into a scientific game of chess with coaches rearranging or maneuvering their men so that a decided gain results. In other words, you must take advantage of a weakness.

Coaches scout each other's team thoroughly and visualize the changes necessary to effect a victory. These modifications are not made until the team in question is your next foe. To make the alterations before you play that particular team eliminates the surprise element and affords them ample time to set up defenses.

Six years ago, Bob Mitten, our chief scout, noticed that Millersville Teachers had their center covering a motion man. The Millersville man was a fine performer, but he lacked the speed of some of our backs. Our head coach, Glenn Killinger, then changed our basic pass patterns. He assigned our fastest back to go in motion on a long count, and then sprint downfield for a pass. God had just not gifted the Millersville center with sufficient speed to match our back, as a result we scored three cheap touchdowns within six minutes of play to ice the game. Without that bit of maneuvering where a lack of speed was exploited by a swift man, an easy game could have been a difficult one.

3. Surprising Them

The word "surprise" alludes to a condition of unawareness, unexpectedness, and this is exactly what you as a coach aim to produce.

You surprise an opponent when you suddenly utilize some new formation during a game.

A spread or a basic deviation from your normal alignment causes consternation and astonishment. Oklahoma ran from a semi-spread in last year's Sugar Bowl and its opponent, Duke, ran from a bastard short punt formation. Certainly coaches can adjust defenses to the new contrivances, but it must be admitted that players have had no opportunity to practice defending against them. Thus, you are compelled to win a certain game with a defense you established on the spur of the moment.

Having men pass who have never thrown the ball previously, and men kick who have never punted in any of the earlier games, can be an upsetting surprise.

In 1930, I witnessed a great Notre Dame team run rough-shod over Pennsylvania, with Marty Brill scoring four touchdowns. Up to the Penn game, Brill very seldom ran the pigskin. He blocked while Marchie Schwartz took care of the running chores. Penn's defenses were surprised when Brill ran and Schwartz blocked.

Two years ago West Chester defeated a powerful Delaware team on the strength of a quick kick maneuver inserted by Coach Killinger. Jackie Wendland, our left half, did the quick kicking from a basic "T" alignment. It proved to be a tremendous offensive weapon and made possible a great victory.

Imagination a Common Denominator

There is a common ingredient to be found in all three devices. It is identified as imagination. Imagination determines the quality and trend of your thoughts. A coach who lacks an imaginative mind simply cannot develop this strategy. Judgment and reason on the gridiron have little vigor, save for the realization which the imagination gives to them. You must visualize tactical changes in the deployment of your players just as clearly as an architectural plan proclaims the design of a structure. A definite pattern of changes must emerge from your creative thinking. Most important of all, the ultimate result of your imagery should be worthwhile because it is tailored to your material. It is imperative that whatever innovations you insert must be functional.

It would be prudent to go about the task of installing the new alignments with a prediction of success. It cannot—must not— be a mere expression of hope. Before the kickoff, every member of your squad should be convinced that with the new tactical weapons, he cannot miss.

Intelligence Another Necessary Ingredient

Johnny Boyd, an outstanding high school coach from Atlantic City, New Jersey, once said, "Football is ninety percent perspiration and ten percent inspiration. How do you inspire a dummy?" No truer words were ever spoken. If you, as coach, improvise new variations your squad should have the intelligence for their implementation, otherwise you are wasting time. The results of your fertile imagination will vary in direct proportion to your squad's I.Q.

BE CHAMPS

All outstanding coaches want their football players to think in terms of winning championships. When you have players who develop a real pride in being champs, they are always tough to lick. They will never fold, and the opposition will have to kill them inch by inch. This type of team dies hard.

I recently listened to my neighbor Jack Yohe, who formerly

coached Bloomsburg State Teacher's College, explain the word "Champs" by breaking it down into its component parts and then defining each letter.

C. . . . Concentration
H. . . . Heart
A. . . . Attitude
M. . . .Modesty
P. . . . Practice
S. . . . Sacrifice

Concentration

You have evidence of concentration when you ask a player to drill *once* and he does it a *hundred* times to gain adroitness, instead of asking a *hundred* times in order that he will do it *once*.

Concentration means being absorbed, drowned in his work, because of the overwhelming desire to succeed. It includes focusing his entire personality on the project until he is lost. He becomes oblivious to everyone and everything said about him. All of his energies, conscious and unconscious, are marshalled for one single purpose—the task at hand.

I have known football players who, at a coach's suggestion, have gone out on the practice field all alone and worked for hours. Tex Flannery, one of my punters, would take the bag containing practice footballs, stand at midfield, and kick twelve balls toward the coffin corner—then retrieve them and repeat the process for a solid hour. The fact that he was alone mattered little, for the desire to punt well had mastered his soul completely.

Heart

It takes a lot of heart to continue to play football in the face of adversity and defeat. Some players are frontrunners and excel only when they are ahead. The real hallmark of a champion is his ability to come back—to come from behind.

Five years ago, we lost to East Stroudsburg Teachers because one of our ends failed to contain an end run. That blunder was one of the deciding factors in our loss. This man was broken-hearted, because it was the first loss to the opponent in 16 years. The important item was not that we lost, but that the heart this end possessed manifested itself in his refusal to quit. During his senior year, while playing against the same East Stroudsburg team, he acquitted himself like an All-American. He was a bear-cat on defense, covered punts like a blanket, scored two touch-downs on passes, and blocked a punt for another. He had heart. He had come back.

This past season, our center, Dick Borkowski, injured his shoulder in the Drexel game. He couldn't raise his arm for a week. By the time our game with New Haven arrived, the doctor ordered a special piece of equipment and said it would be safe to use him if we wished. Coach Killinger never plays an injured man regardless of the anticipated outcome of the game. On the sidelines during the first quarter, Borowski gave me no peace until I finally put him in. Strangely enough, the shoulder didn't bother him at all, despite the savageness of the play, but imme-diately after the game the intense pain returned. Borkowski's smile of satisfaction at having participated all but blotted out the hurt. Borkowski wasn't very big, but he was all heart.

Attitude

In group athletics good attitude is displayed when players surrender their own personal accomplishments for a successful team effort.

Last season I watched Kenny Alston beat out a three-year veteran for the right end position. The veteran was extended to play the best ball of his career but it still wasn't good enough to retain his old post. The younger man had come, and would not be denied.

It was heartwarming to observe these two practicing together, helping each other perfect skills, knowing all the time that with a gain in proficiency one would lose his job.

As I evaluate last year's undefeated team, many incidents stand out, but none bigger than the veteran tapping the rookie on the rump before the opening kickoff and saying—"Let's go, Ken, I'm rooting for you, buddy." That feeling was genuine—

for the man had somehow learned to lose himself in place of West Chester.

Modesty

Michigan State's Duffy Dougherty said at a banquet in his honor, "You know, it took me only ten years to become a success overnight." How true, for during the last ten years he was an unknown assistant coach, then a head coach saddled with a losing season. Then came the Big Ten Championship followed by a victory in the Rose Bowl—suddenly he became a gigantic core of influence, adulation, and admiration. What a bounce of a football will do! As a winning coach nothing should turn your head; modesty must reign.

Twelve years ago, West Chester enjoyed its first undefeated season. Coach Killinger, while being honored at a testimonial dinner, reminded his audience that he enjoyed an all-victorious season on the strength of one point. A 7-6 victory over Millersville. It was amusing to see him hold up one finger and state, "I want all to know that one point is the small difference between me and a lot of other coaches. It isn't a very big spread, and any one of the other coaches could just as easily be standing here tonight."

Modesty also implies keeping your sense of proportion, regardless of local or national acclaim. A story about Knute Rockne demonstrates this clearly.

By 1929 Notre Dame had been established as a world football power. Everywhere they played, thousands of people cheered them on. The turnstiles clicked, so much so that the administration realized enough funds to build a new stadium. In 1930 the field was to be named and dedicated. Father Cavanaugh, the president, called Rockne into his office and said, "Rock, we plan to dedicate the new stadium. I have decided upon a name." The little Norwegian said, "Wonderful, what is it?" President Cavanaugh said, "We shall call it Rockne Field, because you have contributed so much toward its completion." Rockne got up and paced the floor as he did in the dressing room before a game, turned to the president, and said, "Father, there is only one name befitting that construction and that is the Stadium of Notre Dame. No coach can ever be bigger than an institution without losing his sense of proportion."

To this day that arena is known as the Notre Dame Stadium. A more modest man never lived.

Practice

"Nothing succeeds like success" is a well known axiom but its corollary, "Nothing fails like failure," carries more impact.

Practice is the means presented to an aspiring athlete to perfect the skills in which he lacks mastery. To indulge in a routine wherein he already possesses efficiency at the exclusion of developing those he lacks is shortsightedness.

Young athletes must condition themselves to spend the major portion of practice time in converting their weak points into strong ones.

Years ago, Ted Williams, one of baseball's greatest hitters, continued to pull the ball to right field, despite an overshift which had left field unattended. Shrewd baseball managers knew he had not mastered the art of hitting the ball to the opposite field.

Ted Williams was too intelligent and too fierce a competitor to allow this to go on. The following season, when Boston met Cleveland, the Williams shift was soon in evidence. Left field was wide open. The "Splendid Splinter" immediately hit a double down the left field line. To prove it was no fluke, he repeated the action the next time at bat.

What sports writers failed to mention in their columns, was that Ted Williams spent a great portion of spring training practicing hitting the ball to the opposite field.

Because his weak point was converted into a strong asset, Williams was not only doubly dangerous, but increased his contribution to the entire ball club.

Sacrifice

In earlier chapters "paying the price" was discussed. Anything worth doing is worth doing well. In order to do this, athletes must make sacrifices. It will be necessary to give up dates, parties, and even renounce fast friends.

In practicing football, the athlete has added another activity to his life. This involves time. With the 24 hours in a day remaining constant, he simply cannot do everything he indulged in previous to going out for football. If he does, he is stealing a little time from each activity and a loss in efficiency will result. It is imperative that he give up some of the other extra-curricular activities. This requires sacrifice. You must compel him to put into practice the principle "Mature men do the things they do not like to do."

All of the above when combined spells "CHAMPS."

RESULT OF WINNING

Mixed Emotions

A winning coach must understand that he will be received with mixed emotions. He will be admired, respected, loved, and hated, and they do not always balance.

After every win, praise will multiply. You will be like a relay runner who gets an extra baton to carry every lap, instead of passing on the one he has. In your case, the only difference is that each victory becomes a baton of prestige and authority. Your lights will really begin to shine.

On the other hand, you will also be running the gauntlet of unpopularity, suspicion, and rancor, in the minds of those whose teams you have defeated. All the world does not love a winner. Ugly rumors about your personal coaching techniques, the school's low academic standards, and your soft schedule will be circulated. You soon will conclude that football is a great tragedy, regardless of whether you win or lose.

Popularity a Matter of Geography

Distance becomes the key factor in your popularity when enjoying a winning season. You must keep uppermost in mind that the higher you soar, the smaller you look to those you have left behind.

In your own immediate area—your school and community—
you bask in unlimited popularity. You could run for any office,
from mayor to dog-catcher, and be elected by an overwhelming
majority.

However, over in that other domain, which your opponents
call home, your popularity chart takes a sharp dip. Fellow
coaches question your methods and opposing players rationalize
their defeat by punching holes in your success. They constantly
point out how one insignificant run or pass was the turning point
in their loss. Really, you were lucky—it could have gone either
way.

There is still a great deal of territory left outside your locale
and that inhabited by your opponents. It is in this vicinity, this
outer rim, where you achieve your biggest glory.

To these people, by whom results of games are judged in an
impersonal manner, you emerge a hero, one who exemplifies
everything that is fine and clean in American athletics. In this
area you have stature. They believe that you, as coach, are
unexcelled as a builder and leader of youth.

A HUMBLE ENDING

Most stories eulogizing someone start with his humble beginning. When writing of winning coaches, "humble ending" looms
more importantly.

A coach must possess dignity and humility. These qualities
must not be an obvious act nor simply a veneer. They should be
genuine and sincere. As coach, you must remain completely un-
affected by your sudden success. It is wise to remember that the
greatest magnifying glass in the world are a coach's own eyes
when they look upon his person.

When you are being exalted and proclaimed as the area's outstanding coaching personality, do not forget that with the
bounce of a football, a single point, or even one yard either
way, some other coach would be in your chair acknowledging
the plaudits.

At the Atlantic City Clinic, I had the pleasure of meeting Jess
Dow, of New Haven State Teachers College, who enjoyed an

undefeated record in 1956. One of his victims was West Chester. This past season he had a mediocre record. One of his most humiliating losses was suffered at the hands of our own aroused West Chester team. The New Haven game was the springboard to an undefeated season for us.

It was amusing to hear Dow say, "Jim, how did you folks get so smart and me so stupid in one year?"

Share the Wealth

When you address high school and college athletes at the many dinners which spotlight you as the guest speaker, be careful not to speak *twice* before you think *once*. A wise coach will share the wealth of prestige which the season has produced.

Your humility should compel you to say that your contributions were unimportant. You should clothe your talk in a garment which covers your assistants, players, the faculty and administration with glory.

Tell your audience it seems almost unbelievable that so many ministering angels were close by to bring you through a winning season. Your "I's" must never be too close together.

By acclaiming everyone else and his valuable contributions you add honor to your person.

Never Knock

As a coach of a winning team, do not be so carried away with flattery so that you unconsciously knock the opposition. Flattery is like cologne; it should be smelled, not swallowed. When questioned about another coach or team, always cast the universal blanket of "Good" over them. You become preeminently great only when you develop a tolerance for the performances of less gifted men. Never indulge in the practice of looking down at your weaker colleagues.

Thanking God

As a coach I have never been obsessed with religious fanaticism, but have always possessed a profound, fundamental belief in God. Man never accomplishes anything alone. Before every game I stop at any nearby church to spend a quiet moment with God the Almighty.

The first thing the Pilgrims did when they touched Plymouth Rock was to kneel down under the open sky and thank the Lord. That was why they had come here—to meet God in the way they thought right. So have I also entered His House to ask Him to make me worthy of whatever He has planned for me and my squad that day. Because all is not God but God is All, I find comfort in that moment of supplication I share with Him.

Following a defeat or victory I make it a point to enter the dressing room, absent myself from the crowd, and sit silently for a few seconds. In that short span of time I ask God to keep me humble, to keep my mind wise, to forever keep my motives pure, to make me worthy of His Blessing, and above all, to keep me convinced that working with young men is God's will.

> We are not here to play . . . to dream . . . to drift,
> We have hard work to do and loads to lift,
> Shun not the struggle . . . face it . . . 'tis God's gift.

JEERS AND TEARS

coaching during a losing season

Our greatest glory is not in never failing but in rising every time we fall——GOLDSMITH

Objective Realism

If you believe in objective realism, you will accept as inevitable the coming of a time when losses will plague you. Every coach sooner or later experiences this buffet. Nothing matures a mentor faster than a losing season. No sane coach can possibly expect to have winning seasons year in and year out. In coaching, there will be sorrows as well as joys, fulfilled hopes as well as disappointments, maliciously unkind people as well as trustworthy friends. Smooth going will alternate with conflict. Most coaches, despite this realization, strive for balance. They do not want all the bad at one time. Unfortunately for them, however, this sometimes does happen. Over the years a good coach will try to develop a habit of being ready for such an eventuality. My experience has taught me that you always feel the sting regardless of how ready you thought you were. The important thing, nevertheless, is that you do not let it get you down—that you come back and do not alienate any relationships in the process.

The objective of this chapter is not to teach a coach how to

145

adjust to losing, but to find an acceptable method of preventing the continuation of the failure.

THE COACH COMBATS THE LOSSES

The following are some techniques a coach can employ to offset the sting of continual failure.

A New Outlook

When caught in the web of a losing season, and when you are convinced it is not your coaching or the play of your men, then an attitudinal change is necessary. You no longer are the bigot, the autocratic, almost tyrannical, boss described in chapters 1 and 6. The important phase of losing is never to lose the respect and love of your men at this time. A coach can always point to a winning record to offset the buffets of critics, regardless of the source. A losing coach can show nothing to balance the record. He finds himself in a position where his players are the only ones who can save him from the public wrath. The coach must be solicitous, kind, fatherly, and understanding when dealing with his players. He drives them, but is constantly building them up— making them enjoy being driven. It is unnecessary to tear them down, for opponents take care of that at game time. You must repair that damage with kindness during the week.

More Meetings—More Time—More Speakers

I have accomplished this by spending more time with the team. When losing I call more meetings, and talk at length with individual members of the squad. I do this in order to nullify what they hear outside by feeding them my particular philosophy. This also enables me to feel the pulse of the community—to learn what the people are thinking.

I plan get-togethers for the squad at my home. Well-known coaches and sports personalities are brought in to address the men. The fact that so many well known and successful coaches are your friends checks and retards the instinctive desire of your players to lose confidence in you.

Rallies

Losing will cause many public sparks to be fanned, ready to burst into a flame which will be aimed at devouring the coach. You must keep them from exploding. You must survive this scuttling attempt. One well-known herculean method of holding student and public wrath to a minimum is to disconcert them. Any other course is disastrous. You must now be cautious, shrewd, and downright wily. You can accomplish this by having an increased number of football rallies where you are the main speaker.

Your speech to the students appears casual, off the cuff, but you load your talk with carefully placed electrical charges designed to shock pupils into supporting the team, despite the many losses.

Your talk to them is one which challenges them to rally to your cause because they feel sorry for you as a fine personality.

I recall two incidents when I spoke to a student body after the team had lost four straight games. I went before the pupils and in saddened voice, punctuated with many pauses, said, "Friends, I have never spoken to you with as heavy a heart as today. Nothing is going right. I ignore my wife and even snub my little kids. My heart bleeds to stand before you with the record we have. I cannot blame the players. We have the making of the greatest team in the league next season. I don't deserve a gang of players who are as fine and as loyal as this present team. They practice every day as if they were undefeated. No previous team of mine, even in victory, exhibited the spirit of this group. I'm crazy about them. I love them and pray that you will be patient with us as we continue to battle inexperience in our search for victory."

This talk brought more students out to the next game than any other previous contest. Their cheers even in defeat rocked the stadium.

Another device I used was to go before the student body before playing a team I knew would beat us badly and say the following. "This Saturday the hardest-hitting fullback in the

league will be here. The highest-scoring halfback and the biggest
line will be on our field. This Saturday afternoon, an end 6′4″
will line up against Joe Francois who is 5′6″ and only 150 lbs.
Under normal conditions I would call the game off, except that
your team wouldn't permit me. Despite the odds, your team will
show up to do battle. Now I'm here to ask for volunteers. How
many of you will be brave enough to cheer your own team on
in spite of past failures? Those of you with the 'guts' to show up
Saturday and sink or swim with these men before me, please
stand up." Mass hysteria or mass psychology will compel them to
stand. Then proceed to tell them how grateful the men on the
squad are for their support. This device has been successfully
employed by me on numerous occasions, even though it was
ballyhooing a funeral.

A Dressing Room Party

Surprising your squad with a dressing room party after a
Monday practice following a big loss works wonders. I recall
during my La Salle coaching tenure watching my men dress,
following our fourth straight loss. One look at them convinced
me of the need to plan something to pick them up.

I contacted a delicatessen store and ordered two hundred
bricks of ice cream and two hundred cup cakes of mixed variety.
I ordered them to be delivered to the squad's dressing room and
set up at 4:30 P.M. I interrupted practice and called the men
together for a brief meeting on the field. I spoke to the team in
a tone of encouragement; then I sent them in. What a pleasant
surprised awaited them! They dug into the food like hungry
bears, not even bothering to shower. I joined them along with
my assistants, trainers, and managers. It was a most convivial
gathering. The losses seemed forgotten and the same spirit
evinced at the opening of camp prevailed once more.

Purchase New Equipment

A dressing room party is a fine gesture, but by no means a
cure-all for a losing team. Despite this gesture, a team may continue its losing ways—what then? It merely becomes necessary to

resort to other subterfuge to balance the dearth of victories. An added technique is to purchase new equipment—namely, jerseys. This is another method of having the men push the losses in the background by substituting something else to take their place. Surprise them with new jerseys on Wednesday. Have them try them on and take pictures of the squad in their new regalia. This will help remove the sting of another defeat. Buying new jerseys is equal to a woman purchasing a new hat. It gives a lift.

New Plays May Supply a Lift

The many defeats your team has suffered is ample evidence that your plays are inadequate, and perhaps too poorly executed, to produce a victory. Because your men are intelligent enough to arrive at a similar conclusion, it is imperative that you supplement your present repertory of plays with some new formation. The intent is to give your men a new lift, a shot in the arm, new encouragement. It is similar to a new weapon devised for war. It is discouraging for players to run plays which game play has proved sterile and ineffective. Giving them new formations, which are still untried, offers new hope. Practice will be viewed with renewed stimulation, for a new look has been produced to achieve victory.

These alignments are usually "spreads" and are commonly known as "last-resort formations." Coaches employ them when conventional plays and ordinary blocking and tackling fail to produce results. Because they are new and varied, they are difficult to defend against, and often succeed in scoring a token touchdown which will save face in a crushing defeat.

In my first year of coaching at La Salle, I used spreads after our third defeat. We continued to lose badly, but the new formation invariably resulted in a score.

This enabled me to add new variations of the spread for each ensuing game. I found the players liked them and looked forward to practice, despite defeat following defeat.

Call on Your Press Friends

The social devices described are sometimes insufficient, and you must augment them with something new. Nothing is more appealing to an adolescent than seeing his name in print. Because your relationship with the press has been a most cordial and friendly one, it is permissible for you to call on them for a lifting story. Ask them if they can do a story on the assets of the ball club such as spirit and determination, and minimize the liabilities. The story they write should be permeated by the one thought, "Better days are ahead and victory is just over the horizon." This is also the time for your press friends to remind the public of your past coaching successes. If you are new and have no record then your personal outstanding playing achievements should be kept before the players and the public.

Assistants Are Loyal

This is a time when you begin to believe that coaches have many friends and also too few.

I have written of the need to spotlight your assistants, to have them share in whatever credit and glory accrue to you and the team. They must never be sidelined when it comes to giving credit. In writing this, I have a basic reason in mind. A coach cannot spell the word, "brothers," without writing, "others." I have found that if you divide the grandeur and renown of winning with your aides, they will assume a share of any blame when losses are incurred. They cannot help but remain loyal. If, on the other hand, you have been an egomaniac while winning, a profound egotist whose smug self-satisfaction oozed from your every act, you will not win the admiration of your helpers; in fact, you will drive them away. They will glory in your downfall if you follow that routine. The high and mighty has been leveled off, and they will revel in the sight.

A key to remember in handling colleagues is that when you win, you win together, and when you lose, you lose together. This is a time when you need all the friends you can muster, and your assistants should be your friends.

A true assistant is one who knows all the mean, unrespectable, unbecoming, humiliating facts about you. He knows every time you flubbed in coaching strategy, yet he loves you in spite of them. He is the one who picks you up when you fall by refusing to second-guess you. He defends everything you do, even when he personally disagrees with it.

FINDING REASONS FOR FAILURES

Evaluation a Must

When you experience a losing season, there are specific reasons to which this can be attributed. As the victim, you must assume the responsibility of doing some introspecting. You must answer the question "Why?" Once this has been accomplished, a remedial program is initiated.

Basic Reasons for Losing

There are usually four basic reasons why football teams lose:

1. Poor coaching.
2. Inexperienced personnel.
3. Inadequate personnel.
4. Lack of junior high and intramural programs.

POOR COACHING

Take Inventory

Your first undertaking when suffering a poor season should be a personal inventory of your coaching. Despite the emotional climate which accompanies introspection, an honest self-appraisal must be made. Ask yourself, "Where did I fall down?" Evaluate each game separately—the defense—the offense. Could you have avoided the loss? Did you do everything possible? Would you, despite the result, repeat the same game strategy? If you could make too many fundamental changes in your offense and defense, then you are at fault. *You* lost the ball games, not the players. The players merely carried out your plan of doom. Remember, a defeat usually means that your team did the wrong things.

A coach improves not by imagining himself to be perfect, but by acknowledging his limitations and setting out to remove them in a rational manner. That rational manner manifests itself in first admitting to yourself your faults, and then immediately informing the players. Big things are asked of big people.

Do not be ashamed of your mistakes; remember, everybody else made some too. The only coach I heard from last year who declared he was perfect and didn't make a single error, never finished the sentence. The nurse in attendance came into the room and took him away.

Mistakes are valuable if you recognize them, admit them, learn from them and forget them.

Attitudes To Avoid

When losing, there are certain attitudes you should avoid as soon as possible. They are:

1. The attitude that you will not learn anything from others.
2. The attitude that you are right and no one can convince you otherwise.
3. The attitude that you expect to be done an injustice by your colleagues.
4. The attitude that the blame for losing should be focused on some victim.

Do Not Look for a Scapegoat

I know of one coach who informed the press that a loss could be attributed to the poor play of the right tackle, who failed to halt the bread and butter slant of the opponent. Yet that coach never gave that poor lineman a special technique to employ as a combative weapon for that play. Whenever you resort to the practice of making your players your scapegoats, the time has come for you to turn to some other livelihood.

The result of such an act reminds me of the puzzled expression on the face of a twelve year old boy standing before a juvenile judge and being told that what he needed was more I.Q.

Seek Help

Coaching values cannot be assayed in precise units, but they can be viewed in broad outlines, with sufficient clarity to enable one to learn his weak spots. Once a coach locates his weaknesses, his attitude toward them looms as important. You must not permit emotional indulgence to result. You must not settle into despondency. Your findings should not cause such disappointment that inertia and a desire to resign results. A mature coach will salvage what he can and seek help from there.

Charles Steinmetz, the great president of General Electric, once said, "Every discovery is the answer to some question. There are no foolish questions and no man becomes a fool until he has stopped asking them. It is better to question an issue and reach a conclusion than to reach a conclusion without questions."

Help is sought by planning a program of self-improvement. This can be realized in a two-fold manner. First, bring your problem to the attention of a well-known, successful coach and ask his help. I have found coaches to be the most cooperative men in the world. They think nothing of divulging the innermost secrets of their success to anyone, just for the asking.

Attend Coaching Clinics

Further aid results from the attendance of coaching clinics. It is true that, at times, coaches attend clinics and learn nothing new, but you then can feel secure in the knowledge that what you are attempting to do is exactly what everyone else is doing.

The secret of obtaining specific material concerning your problem is to meet the coaching school clinician in the evenings as they mingle with the audience. Get to them and ask them pointed questions which will resolve your difficulty.

In my twenty-five years of coaching, I have attended at least thirty clinics. School athletic journals and magazines carry pages of advertisements explaining the various types of coaching clinics offered throughout the country.

Dr. Scott has the finest coaching clinic I know of; it is held annually in Atlantic City, New Jersey. His clinicians are famous coaches and better than nine hundred coaches attend. (I was a clinician during the 1958 meeting, which was an experience so rich I shall never forget it.)

Keeping Abreast of Coaching Literature

Keeping abreast of the coaching literature in your field is a taxing obligation, but one which all coaches must accept. Check the library for particular publications worthy of notice and absorption. Write to publishing houses requesting information on all new athletic publications.

Certain periodicals designed particularly for coaches should be read regularly. The observant coach will challenge the interest of his players by making all literature available to them too. If possible, have the library set aside a section known as "The Football Corner." During the basketball season, basketball periodicals will replace the football books; in other words, design a corner of the library for books and magazines on the sport in season.

Gloom and Doom

I want to cite two personal experiences which I hope will add clarity to this phase of a fading relationship.

I graduated from La Salle College in 1936 and in March of the same year, Brother Anselm, the College President, signed me to a three-year contract to teach and coach at La Salle College High School. I was most flattered to serve my alma mater in an untried capacity. It was evident that the president had the utmost confidence in me.

When I started in September, I encountered no difficult problems in the classroom, but my football team lost its first three games. Going into the last week of November we still had not experienced the thrill of victory. With one game and no honor at all left to lose I contrived a slanting five man defensive line to halt a good opponent. We lost that game too by the score of 2-0. Following that game, I hit bottom in despondency. I just couldn't believe my players were that poor. The fault must lie within me, I felt. I just didn't have it as a coach. I was beginning to believe the hearsay evidence of the witnesses for my prosecution.

I jumped into my car and drove to the college faculty house, requesting to see President Anselm. When he asked me to be seated, I poured out my heart. In dejected tones I informd him the players could not possibly be that bad. I just didn't have it, and to go on coaching would be an injustice to every man on my squad. He got up from his chair, put his arm around me and said, "Jim, go home and get a good night's rest. You are upset. You are going to win games, but you must be patient. It takes time." Then he asked in passing whether I had seen any college team play whose offense I particularly liked. I responded, "Yes, I saw Hughie Devore's Providence College team play. I liked his ball club." He then casually suggested I write Devore or see him personally and just talk football. That evening I wrote Devore at Providence, and the following week I met with him. I gained a wealth of insight; in fact, his ideas were instrumental in the creation of an entire new offense. The mistake I had made was to have my high school team employ the exact plays I had when in college. I neglected to give attention to the material at hand. I fitted men to the system instead of the system to the material.

The next season we won seven and lost two, despite the loss of seven of the previous year's starting eleven.

In 1951 I suffered through another week of humiliation and shattered confidence. In my present capacity as line coach, I observed West Chester play East Carolina Teachers College in Greenville, North Carolina. They had won twenty-seven straight and possessed an outstanding team. We won 6-4 in a closely contested ball game. We were riding high when we returned to prepare for Delaware University, our next opponent.

Meeting Delaware the following Saturday we suffered the most decisive beating a West Chester team has ever sustained in my twelve years as line coach. They defeated us 46-6 and could have scored a hundred. That night and extending through the next week I was sure I knew nothing about line play. Despite undefeated teams, Little All-Americans and outstanding linemen in the past, I was certain I didn't know even the fundamentals of line play. To watch helplessly as Delaware ran over us shattered all of my confidence. It was an empty feeling, not one of rancor, not of hurt, but just plain bewilderment and surprise. Our line just could not possibly be that poor.

On Wednesday the confusion began to wear off and our head coach Glenn Killinger and I engaged in some sound thinking. We concluded that Delaware had finally solved our gap eight defensive line. They had designed one play that tore it apart at will, and we just could not cope with it. We failed to make defensive adjustments. The players carried out their individual assignments with proficiency but could not cope with Delaware's own scheme. In other words, the players did not lose the game. Our defense did.

We told the men they did not lose the game; the coaches did. Our problem was clear. We had to make adjustments in the defense so future opponents could not exploit us. At first we toyed with the idea of discarding the entire defense, then we recalled its efficiency over a 24 game span and decided to make adjustments and change it once more. The next game it seemed more successful than ever. The changes had made it impregnable.

Losing Can Be a Tonic

Despite the lift one gains from every success, it is important that it be interspersed with failure before it becomes clear what makes for success and what makes for failure. True humiliation, resulting from a loss, carries an important function. It carries discomfort and becomes a valuable spur to do something about losing. When you win, you are content to go on with the same defense and offense—there is really no need to change. A loss, however, is unpleasant, and causes a readjustment of your pattern of play. Change always stems from the irritation of defeat.

It is important to remember that a defeat will always shatter your confidence for a short time, but champions always come back. A loss is a good tonic, as I pointed out in the story of my early coaching career and later, in our Delaware game. Being rocked with a loss gets you well-hammered in the process for the victories which follow. The path to victory is always strewn with losses. Make every mistake teach you a lesson. Fear not a loss.

I remember one of my linemen entering the service following his graduation. I said, "Dick, I plan to follow you in every game," since he had made the Fort Myers football team. He informed me they had a good team and the following Saturday they were to play Jacksonville. I begged him to call me with the results. Sunday morning the phone rang and he said, "Coach, we had a tough game yesterday." I asked, "Did you win?" He replied, "No, we lost 78-0." I ventured, "You didn't lose, you were murdered." He said, "Yes, I know." "Well, one loss doesn't ruin an entire season—cheer up. Who do you play next week?" His answer rolled me off the chair. "I don't know," he replied, "the coaches won't tell us."

Here was a team worse off than any of us. To gain heart, remember that every great team loses, including Notre Dame. Losing isn't common to any particular institution. Sooner or later every club will lose. I remember two drunks entering town after their team lost. One said, "You know we must be getting closer to town—we're bumping into more people." The other suddenly looked up, saw a sign and said, "Hey, there's another team that lost: Hamburger 15—Hot Dog 10."

Take heart in the following proverb. "He that stumbles and falls not quite, gains a step."

The 1957 Notre Dame team did not lick Oklahoma on the day of the game. They licked Oklahoma the previous year, when they were rocked with defeat upon defeat. There the lessons of that victory were learned.

INEXPERIENCED PERSONNEL

Take Your Licking

When losing because of inexperienced personnel, patience is a virtue. You just take your licking on this occasion. You simply cannot hurry experience, for it is a learning process, and learning moves at its own pace. Experience usually results from mistakes. The hope of every coach is that errors will be made in practice, where they will not be so costly; however, there are some aspects of the game which are mastered only during actual game competition.

This is a time when you, as coach, are prepared to lose. Because you do not expect otherwise, you prepare everyone concerned to accept it also.

Understanding and Kindness a Must

While you are beset with losses in the process of waiting for your men to gain the necessary experience, kindness is a must. Each loss you suffer together sows seeds of two or three future victories. Team morale must be kept at a high pitch. You would be very unwise to blame your players. Constantly strive to keep harmony, despite defeat after defeat. The harmony of the squad is composed of the harmony of each individual player.

In the beginning of the season, unless you are a dupe, you should anticipate a losing season. The only time an inexperienced squad realizes many victories is when opponents suffer more from the same defect. This condition is hardly likely. You tell players you expect to lose quite a few games, but that is the price a club pays for the necessary experience. If you do otherwise and deceive your players and the public, you destroy faith. When you are guilty of this, public suspicion will be quick and penetrating. Your hypocrisy will arouse a stinging contempt. You must be honest with the school, community and the press. Tell all, "this is a building year—better seasons are ahead." Tell everyone who will listen that, "Great men were once little men."

The American Fan Is Cruel

During a losing streak you and your players will be exposed to much second-guessing and criticism. It is your self-appointed task as coach to protect your players when losing.

As I look back over my coaching career, it seems to me that it is pretty much of a definite law that some spectators are more prone to notice what is wrong with a team than what is right. During the last twenty-five years some fans have created a hell from which there is no redemption. They have become downright cruel, because they have forgotten what they should have remembered, and remembered what they should have forgotten. Let me give you some evidence of this cruelty. Some fans forget Ruth hit 714 home runs during his fabulous baseball career and remember only that he struck out 1,320 times; more than anyone else.

Some have forgotten that Cy Young was the winningest pitcher in baseball with 511 victories. They recall only that he lost more games than anyone else.

Is Roy Reigles' claim to fame the fact that he was an All-American Center, an inspirational leader who led his team into the Rose Bowl? Many fans have forgotten those accomplishments, and to this day remember him as "Wrong Way Reigles." During the heat of battle he picked up a fumble, became confused, ran the wrong way, and lost the ball game for his team. Some fans are cruel.

Ralph Branca is not always remembered because he helped pitch the Brooklyn Dodgers to two pennants. His claim to fame is one pitch which Bobby Thompson hit out of the park to win the pennant for the New York Giants.

It Can Happen to You

Now your lot will be no different. When you lose, you become a live target for every critic in town. In some localities, the fans will even go so far as to exhibit raw passion when talking about you. No man in any other profession will be more attacked, defended, explained, obscured, and slandered. Throughout all of this your ulcers get ulcers, but you quiet them. You restore the confidence of your players by patting them on the back and hold out for a brighter tomorrow. This requires a real toughness—tough enough to meet all obstacles in stride. Coaching, some one said, is an obstacle race. As a coach your integrity and character must never wane when you lose.

I like the comment which Birdie Tebbetts, the former Cincinnati manager, was supposed to have made during last year's baseball season, when Cincinnati went from a pennant contender to fifth place in eight days. Redleg fans were so angry that they

hanged Manager Tebbetts in effigy. When he was informed of
their doings he said glumly, "If I'd been there, I'd have helped
them."

Jack Dempsey, as champion, never endeared himself to the
American public until he lost his title to Gene Tunney in 1926.
On meeting his wife, Estelle Taylor, she asked what had happened. Between swollen lips he announced, "Honey, I forgot to
duck." No excuses, no defenses, these men took their licking like
real Americans.

Tommy Hitchcock

When suffering defeat upon defeat, it becomes a momentous
task to salve the ego of your players. I found dividends in re-
telling the story of Tommy Hitchcock, the great polo player. Before he went overseas, where he was later killed, he is reported
to have said to his boy, "Son, win as though you were used to it
and lose as if you liked it."

Football, in order to have a residual value, must teach people
how to lose and bounce back. Winning is only half the game.
Today, too much is made of winning and the other element is
ignored completely. In this age of Sputniks, winning or losing a
football game is as unimportant as a speck of dandruff falling
on this huge earth of ours.

In an age when our children's children could be cremated
equally instead of created equally, losing a ball game is compara-
tively unimportant when compared to how it was played.

Losing Proves Loyalty

To lose and come back for more requires real "guts." It is easy
to win. To report for practice day in and day out with no victory
to buoy you requires a real man. Men who keep coming have
proven their loyalty. Loyalty is no problem with winning teams.
without it a team can't be a winner for long—and losing teams
without loyalty will not get back into the win column.

A young father, baby-sitting with his eleven-year-old son, was
being driven frantic by the boy's actions. To solve his problems,
he cut a map of the United States out of a magazine and cut it

up into a hundred smaller pieces. Calling his son he said, "Joey, how smart are you? Can you put this map together? I'll bet you can't." The youngster went to work and in twenty minutes the map was once again in one piece. The father, who envisioned a two hour job, and then bed, was amazed. He asked the boy how he was able to piece it all together so quickly. The boy replied, "There was a picture of a man on the other side of the map. I knew if I put the man together right, that the country would come out all right, too." How true; if your young players come out all right, the country will too.

My college coach often repeated the words he once heard the famous Will Rogers utter at Notre Dame rally. Rogers expressed great admiration for the Notre Dame teams because, "You met success like gentlemen and disaster like men.."

Tell your men that their losses will eventually come to an end because you know that, as their coach, you will not permit them to become used to losing.

I remember vividly watching an entire green West Chester team playing a seasoned Bloomsburg Club in 1954. Head Coach Killinger realized only too well that only three months previously these young men were performing in high school. Playing college ball was a big jump. The pressure of opposing a traditional opponent, plus inexperience, resulted in numerous elementary mistakes. At one stage of the game Jackie Wendland, a freshmen back, was sucked out of position and a cheap enemy touchdown resulted. When the back was pulled out minutes later, Coach Killinger greeted him at the side line with an enthusiastic handshake followed by the remark, "O.K. boy!—this shall pass—we're learning." That year we suffered four defeats but have lost only one game in the three ensuing seasons. The same team which took their lumps as freshmen have played like champions since. I like to think the encouraging words paid dividends.

Only Once

It must be clear to you, as coach, that fans will only once accept your rebuilding program with patience. The average fan is quite an intelligent one. He knows that you are losing certain

key men through graduation, therefore, he expects you to play
new men with the intent of giving them the necessary experience
to eventually replace the seniors. As coach of a team in the throes
of a losing season you would be foolish to play seniors. It is impossible to give experience to seniors, so lose without them. It is
more efficient to lose with sophomores than with seniors, so play
the sophomores whenever possible.

Fans are much more understanding when injuries to key men
hurt you than when you use the "lack of experience" line to
explain losses.

Victory Is Never Cheap

Of course it is distressing to see your teams lose, but the fact
that some day the losing will terminate is encouraging. Arguments are useless where facts are sufficient. What can you say
about a team that is losing because it lacks the "know-how?"
The only consolation which accrues to you is the knowledge that
when victories do come, they will be glorious ones. The anticipated victories will not be cheap ones and players will never
hold or view them lightly.

Don't Let Failure Go to Your Head

This is an old expression used to describe a coach who rationalizes his losses in order to find some measure of comfort. You
are guilty of this when you count the first downs your team made,
as compared to the few of the winning team. You point to the
many passes your team completed, the fumbles recovered, the
few penalties suffered in defeat. Citing the good points of the defeat makes you appear happy. You have convinced yourself that
your team won everything but the ball game. When this has taken
place, failure has gone to your head.

Losses Will Sap Your Strength

There will come a time when you practically fall into a coma.
Everything you eat will taste like raw cabbage. You will go to
bed tired and wake up fatigued. Jokes no longer seem funny to

you. Friends leave you to your own ugly thoughts. You wonder
if you can face another day. It is especially tough on your wife.

Years ago I attended a baseball luncheon where I heard
Charlie Grimm, who managed the Milwaukee Braves, tell this
story. It concerned a skipper fired in September for finishing in
last place. Despondent and discouraged, he and his wife left
town. He drove in sullen silence for 200 miles. Finally his wife
spoke up. "Honey, I'm hungry. Can't we stop somewhere for a
sandwich?" "Shut up, you chatterbox," he snapped, "You're
driving me crazy."

INADEQUATE PERSONNEL

Bear Hunting with a Fishing Rod

The third cause for losing may be inadequate personnel. In
this instance you have gone bear hunting with a fishing rod. You
simply do not have the tools to do the job. This situation is most
trying. Your toughest job here is to face up to what is. The stuff
just isn't there to win ball games against the type of competition
your schedule presents. If you find yourself in this predicament
you have two outs. First, you resign from your present position;
look for a new assignment, because there just isn't anything you
can do to remove the dark stain of defeat from the athletic fabric.
The other alternative is a change in schedule. Play teams commensurate with your type of material.

Remain Emotionally Stable

The season will drive you insane. It is tough to continue to
lose, tougher to watch a club that is doomed, but you take defeat
in stride. Once you have evaluated the situation, you keep your
peace. Do the best you can with what you have. Don't pop off
or look for a scapegoat. You must be emotionally stable and act
professional despite the criticism. If it becames necessary to take
your own part—do it with dignity, courage and in good taste.

Avoid engaging in a common practice used by some older
coaches. It seems that when things do not go right, when they

are in trouble and when they are in doubt, they run in circles screaming and shouting. This "hootin' and hollerin' " will only alienate your assistants, players, and friends. The opposite action is much more appropriate. Say nothing, for I have found that any public treatment always worsens the problem.

Placing the blame on others is much more satisfying than admitting your own deficiency. This trick is as old as the hills. An early illustration of it took place when Adam blamed Eve after he was caught eating the forbidden fruit, and Eve in turn blamed it on the serpent.

The advantage of losing with sophomores already has been presented; you will have them back for two more years. As a prudent coach, therefore, do not offend these players, with this sleight of hand performance, of blaming them for failures. If you want them back for the remaining two seasons you would be wise to keep them as happy as you possibly can under the distressing circumstances. Do not destroy what you value most—your men..

LACK OF JUNIOR HIGH AND INTRAMURAL PROGRAMS

Junior High Athletics Should Be a Varsity Feed

Losing teams hasten the need for developing a football program in the junior high school.

This program to be efficient must include inter-junior high school competition. Properly conducted and supervised, it will be a feed for varsity sports and insure the continuation of successful sporting events.

There is in some quarters today considerable opposition to the inclusion of football on the junior high level because it involves bodily contact. It is often felt that students of this age are too immature for such an activity. It has been my observation that junior high school teams well equipped and coached, and playing teams of similar size, gain from the experience more than is lost. Junior high school athletics should be conducted and patterned after the high school interscholastic program. This teaches participants respect for authority and prepares the young men for varsity competition later on.

Intramural Programs in High School

Intramurals are organized for the purpose of extending the opportunity of team participation. The more men who participate in intramural athletics, the greater will be your chance of realizing a successful interscholastic program. This plan becomes a laboratory of playing skills which later are to be employed in varsity play.

Another advantage of an intramural program is that it takes care of some candidates who lack readiness and who are too little. This program takes up the slack and affords everyone the right to compete, regardless of size or degree of skill. No one will be denied the opportunity to participate and this is a natural re-assignment for the players you were compelled to cut from your varsity squad.

The late President Franklin Roosevelt wrote that "great athletic spirit stems from widening the base of participation. Every boy and man should be encouraged to take part in some vigorous outdoor game. It is far more important for a man to play something himself, even if he plays it badly, than to be just a spectator at someone else's competition."

Because of the exorbitant price of equipment and the coaching problem, intramural football must of necessity be of the "touch football" variety.

Organizing Intramural Touch Football

The finest intramural football program is one in which teams are organized within class years. The entire ninth grade should comprise one league—the tenth graders and eleventh graders separate leagues, too. It is useless to organize a senior class league because they have no eligibility left. If the seniors wish to organize for recreational and competitive purposes, all well and good, but they cannot be a feeder for your program.

The homeroom should serve as the basis for the intramural class league. The advantage of this organization is that the homeroom represents an identified group. A feeling of belonging and association is already there, which makes for good spirit and morale.

The homeroom plan possesses a definite deficiency. It stems from an insufficiency of coaching personnel to handle every homeroom; in fact, some homeroom teachers are women and athletics could be foreign to them. These drawbacks, nevertheless, should not prevent pupils from participating.

At the conclusion of the competition, which will include a schedule of ninth graders playing other ninth graders, tenth graders playing tenth graders and so on, grade champions should be chosen. The competition should stop there.

An important point to remember regardless of the type of unit organization is that all participants are members of the same school, the same family.

Providing Facilities for Intramurals

Some schools object to an extensive intramural program because of a lack of physical facilities such as playing areas. It seems ironic to me that so many schools in this country boast of large, well-cared-for lawns used only as decoration, but little or no outdoor play space. In some communities grass is more important than youth.

Good judgment should be used in selling the school authorities the need for additional space. Above all, do not let a lack of resources kill the program. I suggest, instead, sensible planning to fit the activities to the available and limited area.

HEARTS AND FAILURES

Up to this point losing has been explained when it was inevitable; when there was no possibility at all of achieving victory. There are times, however, when you lose under a different set of circumstances. We will discuss the following topics in the remainder of the chapter:

1. A probable loss to a good opponent.
2. Reaction to this type of loss.

3. Losing to a weak opponent.
4. Reaction to a surprise loss.
5. Losing your first game.

This section will offer a detailed description and evaluation of the relationship and how it varies within the framework of the above environmental conditions.

A PROBABLE LOSS TO A GOOD OPPONENT

There are two techniques which can be employed with considerable success when preparing a team to play an outstanding opponent. They are:

1. Asking for volunteers.
2. Slaughter on the practice field.

Winning or losing hangs in the balance here, so mental attitude could become the deciding factor. Everything you attempt, then, will be geared toward the development of a proper frame of mind. On this particular occasion you have very little to lose. The mere fact that your opponent is formidable is encouraging. Losing to a good team is never humbling, yet defeating a good rival is elevating. Despite all that is written, you are entering the ball game with the knowledge that you could lose, therefore, you wish to take every step possible to prevent it.

Asking for Volunteers

On Monday preceding this game obtain a copy of the players' roster, report to the practice field where you hastily hold a meeting under the goal posts. Tell the squad, "We all realize the calibre of opponent we will be meeting on Saturday. According to the press, friends and everyone in general we are expected to lose. Because this assignment is a big one and beyond the call of ordinary duty, I am going to ask for volunteers. I don't want girls. This is the only game girls have not invaded. I want ball players with real 'guts,' not 'stumble-bums.' Anyone who feels he wants out, now is the time for it. I will not castigate nor criticize you if you do not wish to play this Saturday. A supreme effort is a must. The men I want to play this week must play better than their best, because they sincerely believe they can win. Anyone not sharing that opinion should turn in his uniform. Instead of calling for volunteers as I originally had planned, I will call the role and give each man the opportunity to make his own personal decision." You then proceed to read the names from the players' roster. "Borkowski, do you want to play Saturday? If so, move to the other side of the goal posts." As you read each player's name and he responds in the affirmative, have him join Borkowski. In all my years of coaching I have yet to have a man refuse to play. It will be interesting to observe each candidate join his teammates on the other side of the goal posts and be greeted with a spontaneously enthusiastic reception as he joins the crusade.

Their efforts that week will amaze you. You can overwork this question, addressed to a play not putting out during the week. "Jones, do you want out? It isn't too late. I refuse to have you practice like this, if you expect to play Saturday. Remember, it was your decision. Do you want to change your mind?" Applying this kind of needle throughout the practice sessions will result in building up the necessary tension and by game time you will have a group of wildcats on your hands.

Slaughter on the Practice Field

This situation presents a golden opportunity for the coach firmly to stress game fundamentals. Since everyone expects you to lose and you partially share that opinion too, you turn to fundamentals. For the first three days of the week, engage in long scrimmage sessions. The scrimmages are held under game conditions. You drive the men with a lashing whip as you pound them physically with blocks and tackles. The second day you explain your philosophy and objectives by stating, "You men are supposed to get killed Saturday, so we will do it ourselves. We won't wait till game time. Those of you who survive cannot be killed, and you will be the ones who will play."

You will be surprised at the results the scrimmages will produce. Your players will show anger, but not resentment, toward you. They will develop a hatred for their opponents and will be determined to make them pay for the pains suffered during stepped up scrimmages. This treatment almost invariably results in your team playing a good game. *You never go wrong stressing fundamentals.* Before the week is three days old your men are beginning to meet the challenge by vowing to each other "Lincoln High won't kill anyone!"

But exercise extreme caution not to overwork them, for this will cause them to leave their game on the practice field.

Reacting to This Type of Loss

If you lose despite the employment of the two stated techniques, a special approach to your men is now necessary. You owe a particular loyalty to this kind of team. This is a situation where the continued efforts of you and your men just aren't enough. It is essential for you to cushion the loss for them.

Immediately after the game, enter your locker room and shake hands with every man who played. Offer a word of sympathy, kindness and understanding with each handshake, then stand on a dressing bench and ask everyone not connected with the team to leave. When you and your men are alone, tell them how proud you are of them. Even victory could not add to your personal esteem for every man who played. Tell them how badly you feel for them, because their valiant efforts every day of the last week did not culminate in a victory.

Remind them that they lost to a good team, and some of the breaks went against them, but that they were never outfought. Again emphasize how proud you are to be their coach despite the loss. Help and encourage your players. Losing this type of game usually draws a squad closer together and develops real friendship. Friendship made in adversity and failure sometimes outlasts those made in success. Help them retain faith.

In other words, do all you can to ease the pain and anguish of their loss. Remember, you have another game the next week and these same men will be playing for you.

THE SURPRISE LOSS

Losing to a Weak Opponent

It is always a shocking surprise when you lose to a team you should have defeated. All good coaches take steps to prevent such an occurrence.

When playing this calibre of opponent a special coach-player relationship exists. Playing a good team in itself provides sufficient stimulation; on the other hand, when meeting a weak team, coaches must resort to artificial motivation. Complicating matters is the fact that your men can read, which makes them realize the weak record compiled by the opposition.

During every practice session, you remind your squad that upsets are a misnomer. Whenever a weak team defeats a stronger foe, a letdown made it possible. Tell them their press clippings cannot win the next game for them. The men they are playing do not subscribe to daily papers.

Remind them that they are a good team and it will bring tremendous prestige to this poor opponent should they upset them. Any time eleven men meet eleven men, anything can happen.

When this type of pleading fails to produce the desired result, you resort to subterfuge.

Chase Your Squad

I have experienced much success with the following scheme to help teams whose complacency was hurting them.

On the Thursday before the game I explain my plan to my assistant coaches so as not to interfere with their practice schedule. It will be necessary that they crowd their time in order to be a part of the collusion.

The practice will get under way as usual. Individual work will proceed as planned, with the exception that the tempo will be accelerated. This permits the squad to run dummy scrimmage fifteen minutes earlier. This all should be unnoticed by any member of the team. During the dummy scrimmage you drive them. You castigate them for lack of hustle. Nothing they do is

going to satisfy you. The psychological moment has now arrived. You suddenly scream, "I could run that play faster, and
I'm an old man. You men don't want to play football. Everybody in! Get out of my sight. I don't want to associate with men
who won't put forth 100 per cent effort every day. Go on in!"

The important factor to remember when applying this technique is that you and your aides have attained all your objectives before dismissing the squad.

You and your assistants should not permit any player to remain on the field. Chase them all in. The coaching staff remains
on the field for a short interval then enters the dressing room in
unison, ignoring the squad completely.

Their first reaction will be one of shock, followed by surprise.
As they leave the field their facial expressions will mirror their
disturbance. Their method of departure will furnish you with
evidence of their mental attitudes. Those who run in are merely
putting in time and you have failed to reach them. Those who
walk in dejectedly are those who will come out with renewed
determination tomorrow.

There is no guarantee that this explained plan will produce
a victory, but it will result in a new game attitude. Should a loss
occur despite your pre-game efforts, a definite course of action
is in order.

Reaction to a Surprise Loss

The relationship which follows a surprise loss is unique.

Immediately after the game you enter the dressing room,
ignoring everyone. You utter not a word. Silence reigns and you
register total dissatisfaction and disapproval with the entire ball
club.

Avoid talking or bawling anyone out. It is a cardinal rule not
to discuss the game with your team after they have lost. You
always wait until the following Monday. To talk to a team which
is emotionally upset is pure folly. The sting of the surprise licking is too fresh in their minds to absorb any constructive criticism.

On Monday when they report for practice you really ream

them. You tell them they didn't get licked—they licked themselves. Your previous tolerance must now give way to firmness. You should be a madman as you direct a practice which stresses fundamentals. Regardless of how well they block and tackle that day, nothing should satisfy you. You have made up your mind to that before you dressed for practice. This treatment is repeated Monday, Tuesday, and Wednesday. On Thursday you must begin to build them up by showing satisfaction and complimenting them on their coming back. Games are not won the day of the game but during every practice session preparing to play.

LOSING YOUR FIRST GAME

One Swallow Does not Make a Summer

Every coach hopes for the best at the opening of every season. Coaches need this optimism to come back for more year after year. Good coaches may cry the blues to the press but inwardly they kindle the hope of the good things to come. Winning the opener is always a lift. It puts your mark on the right side of the ledger, and is usually the springboard to more victories.

Losing the opening game, however, is always depressing, not only to the coach, but to the squad as well. Remember, your men have been practicing two to three weeks, morning and afternoon in preparation for this game. All other games require only a week's practice. It is only natural that the sting of defeat suffered in the first game be a prolonged one.

You would be prudent to be sympathetic here; after all, there are nine other games to go. You must not have their confidence shattered so that it takes its toll in the remaining contests. Tell your men, "Forget it, and let's start a new season. One swallow does not make a summer."

chapter nine

HALFTIME RELATIONSHIP

Know something of everything and everything of something—
LORD BROUGHMAN

Time on Your Hands

This is only a fifteen minute relationship, but how you handle it is of extreme importance, for it will have a bearing on the final outcome of the game.

The brevity of the time compels you to be thoroughly organized down to the most minute detail. Every manager and assistant should have a specific assignment to carry out. This frees you to concentrate on the playing mechanisms of your team. The handling of your squad during this short intermisison will vary according to circumstances, some of which follow:

When Winning

When you enter the dressing room at half-time and you are ahead caution them that it is only half over. The score at the end of the game is always the deciding factor.

If they have played a spirited half and have looked good, compliment them. Single out certain individuals for commendation. Show your solicitude for the health of every player by inquiring about injuries. Never play a man who is hurt.

Do not spend more than the first five minutes complimenting

173

them. This allows the men sufficient time to level off and quiet down emotionally so you can make defensive and offensive changes within the next five minutes. The last two minutes should be filled with inspirational talk to pep the team up for the battle in the second half.

When Losing—but Looking Good

There will be occasions when you meet your team at halftime and they are behind in the score but are playing an excellent game. To reprimand them because they are losing is adding insult to injury. If they are playing well, there is really nothing you can do. It is wise to compliment them on their play at this time, too.

The devils in hell will mock you if you transfer shame, scorn, and blame to your team that is playing its heart out yet losing.

Abraham Lincoln once said "A man's legs need only be long enough to reach the ground." Likewise, your adjustments in defense and offense need only be terse ones. They should be made in the bread and butter plays only and should be kept at a minimum. Fifteen minutes to teach an entirely new system of play is much too short. Any changes beyond the necessary ones are superfluous. You must not overcoach.

I have had high school teams behind at half-time by one touchdown. In a calm, collected voice, my parting words to them before they took the field for the second half were, "Two touchdowns will do it, men."

When Losing and Looking Bad

This situation calls for unkind, provoking, devastating, and needling remarks in the early minutes of the half. Your dissatisfaction is made known immediately, because your team is not playing up to its fullest capacity.

It is customary here to pick on one or two men and single them out for carping criticism. Tongue-lash them with a vengeance, being careful never to be personal. You must remember that players do not realize their performances are sub-par.

I want to relate some incidents which took place in my dressing room when I met my squad, after a first half when they were not putting out.

I had a big guard, an average football player, who delighted in popping off all the time. Every week he informed all willing ears what he would do to the coming opponent. Unfortunately for him, he was being driven back on this day and giving away precious yardage. At halftime I walked over to him, placed my nose one quarter of an inch from his, and poured on the abuse. Time compelled me to limit it to one minute. I said, "Jones, you are a little wind blowing hard. You haven't made a tackle all day. You've given away more yardage than the entire line put together. I don't care if you take your uniform off and burn it."

I then turned to his substitute and instructed him to start the half. I took special pains to offer some constructive suggestions to the new player that I knew Jones would pick up too.

As I glanced down the bench, I knew Jones would give his right arm to get back into the fray. I went along with his sub as long as he played well. I then inserted the offending guard with last minute instructions. A renewed effort with increased vigor resulted. This also made the squad indirectly aware of my quickness to make changes, besides giving precious experience to another man.

On another occasion, I had a real scatback who simply refused to blast through the middle of the line. He was a blue streak running outside, but when going up the middle, he would stop. Rival coaches set up defenses to stop the outside and give us the middle. In order to win this game, this man had to blast through the center.

Coming in at half-time I pointed him out for special criticism. I approached him with clenched fists, glassy eyes, and a face reddened with anger. Two feet from him I stopped and began a verbal barrage. "Call yourself a ball player? You can run, punt, pass and sprint when no one is near you, but can you blast a hole through the center? No! When you can do that then I'll say I have a real back who can play for me. Sure we have speed as a team but speed is interpreted not by our fastest man, but by our slow-

est. Smith, you are the slowest man out there." Then I proceeded
to the board and put down the opponent's defense, pointing out
that to win the game we must go up the middle. "If we move
'up the gut,' they will have to take men from the flanks and move
them in—then we can run the ends." I turned to the entire squad.
"I've said my piece. Now go out on that field to hit the middle
or take a licking. I'm not calling the signals. I'm not running
with the ball, Smith is."

Smith became a real back from that moment on.

Collusion at Halftime

In 1940 I accompanied a pretty good La Salle High School
team to play a strong Harrisburg Catholic High. We entered the
dressing room behind, 7-0. I felt we would win the game but
refused to initiate a feeling of complacency by passing that information on to the team.

I spoke with my backfield coach and we agreed on a little
scheme which we hoped would shake them from their lethargy.
After making some changes and helping the men individually in
the mechanics of the game, I tore into them for their lack of
hustle by saying, "You lack hustle; the evidence is overwhelm-
ingly against you. A team is hustling when they are six abreast
covering a kickoff and punt. I have trouble finding one of you,
let alone six. I want gang tackling. I see a ball carrier brought
down and when I begin to count the men who made the tackle,
it is difficult to find more than one. You men aren't hustling." At
the conclusion of my remarks I snatched off my hat and slammed
it to the floor, saying, "I can lick the whole city of Harrisburg all
by myself." With that, Charlie Glenn, my backfield coach, threw
his hat to the floor and said, "I can too." I then sent them back
onto the field.

Of course, this is dramatics and vaudeville moved into the
dressing room, but believe me, it is effective with young people.

Let Assistants Take Over

There have been times when I deliberately stayed away from
the dressing room at half-time, until the last three or four min-

utes. If the proper relationship exists, the mere fact that you, the head coach, are missing, will be a partial motivating factor. In order that the squad not be concerned with your whereabouts and neglect to concentrate on winning, certain steps are necessary. First, you must brief the assistant who will take over. He will inform the squad of your refusal to talk with them. The assistant says, "You men have let him down, and he doesn't deserve it."

Following this, the assistant makes the defensive and offensive suggestions which you passed on to him before the half ended. Your aide is told to complete his talk in approximately 12 minutes. Everything should be quiet, and that is when you make your big entry. Enter the dressing room, look around, walk from one end to the other, then spit on the floor and exclaim, "I thought this was the La Salle dressing room." Without another word you walk out, leaving everything to your assistant, who turns them loose with the following, "Well, you heard it—now let's go."

Hopeless but Helpful

I want to relate another half-time incident which all coaches will meet sometime or another. This is a situation beyond your control, but you can capitalize on it to stir up other playing members. I recall a bread-and-butter halfback named Shaefer, on whose elusive running the success of the entire ball club depended. This particular day he lacked his usual break-away speed. At half-time I inquired what was wrong with him; "I never saw you so slow and sluggish." He replied that he felt sick. Now, this just can't be helped. The man is not to blame; nevertheless, you make much of it. You repeat, "Sick, sick, sick; get sick Christmas, the Fourth of July, Easter, but not in the middle of the biggest game on our schedule." With that, you turn to the squad and tell them everyone must play a little harder to take up the slack.

I remember Shaefer coming to me after the game and apologizing for being sick. I put my arm around him and in a fatherly tone said, "Chick, forget it; those things cannot be helped. Now let's get well so you can help us next Saturday."

A Bit of Halftime Humor

Pieces of humor which took place in some of my halftime talks may be helpful. La Salle was playing Gratz High School, which had a fast break-away halfback named Duchin. All week I had worked on defenses to stop him. I gave particular instructions to a defensive halfback named Moore, who was to watch Duchin and play him man for man.

At halftime, although we were leading by the score of 28-6, Duchin got behind Moore to score a touchdown. During the half-time talk I demanded to know Moore's whereabouts, for I could not see him. He answered, "Here." I turned to him and said, "Moore, all week I cautioned you to watch Duchin—watch Duchin—watch Duchin, and what did you do?" He answered, "I did, coach, and boy, can he run!"

Of course, everyone laughed, including me. It had a loosening effect on the men, and since the game was practically won, the humor was in good taste.

Personalized Humor

Players always find it amusing when the coach blurts out something about a player which he had no idea the coach knew. The information is usually centered around one of their girl friends.

During the half of an easy game, I wowed my men, especially Frank Hoffman, a guard, with these remarks, "Frank, you really are putting the pressure on their passer. You're all over the guy and he can't hit a ball in the tail with a paddle. Keep it up. The only other time I have seen you run as hard was the other night when I spied you holding that little blonde's hand. You were escorting her around like she was a balloon and was going to pop." I took time here to do a caricature of the man. "Boy! I never saw a guy vanish so fast. I came around the corner and bingo! The next time I looked up you were gone—and she was too."

Another opportunity presented itself when one of my good backs stumbled and followed it with a fumble. Once again the score permitted me to be a punster and inject a bit of wit. I said, "Gibbons, your feet aren't mates. You have two left legs. Tomorrow I'm going to paint handles on that football for you."

A coaching point to remember is that if the game can be wrapped up during the first half, humor is appropriate. Your men will almost come to expect it. On the other hand, when things are going badly, every moment must be devoted to making changes and lashing them verbally to get them up.

The Key to Half-time Relationship

The 15 minute intermission was instituted for two reasons: to rest the players, and to give the coaches time to make adjustments so that a more competitive game results. Everything else being equal, a team should play its best ball during the third quarter.

Half-time was never meant to be a place for purely destructive criticism. Some coaches, and even the public, think the turning point of a game can stem from the "hootin' and hollerin' " of a coach. Believe me, it takes more than just building up a head of steam. Certainly, you bawl men out, you criticize, scream, beg, cajole, threaten, sympathize, flatter, and commend, some time or another throughout the season. When you are finished with these preliminaries, you must be sure you have helped your men play better by giving them definite instructions.

I have known coaches who were responsible for losing games. The damage they inflicted during the half-time far outweighed what their opponent did on the field. In reviewing my career, I confess to being guilty of losing games which we should have won, because I neglected to supply the necessary directions.

By all means, work your men up emotionally when the occasion demands, but above all, supply them with the necessary help.

A FINAL WORD ON LOSING

Losing is a humbling experience. You, as a coach, can never

feel exalted until you know the feeling of being humbled. One cannot recognize good without having known bad, even if the latter is a vicarious experience.

Losing must never be an objective. We rationalize when we try to make it so. But because there must be losers if there are to be winners, we must learn to lose with grace.

Brilliant Failures

A good coach uses psychology to make his loss appear brilliant. He first finds something outstanding to talk about despite his loss. When his own team cannot supply a subject he should turn to his victorious opponents and sing the praises of one of their outstanding men. He should make his opponents look so good that it would have been next to impossible to have defeated such superlative performers.

Using Reverse Rationalization

Whenever a coach wins, he rationalizes, so as not to appear boastful. When losing, he turns the tables and engages in reverse rationalization. He states that Roosevelt's loss to Lincoln High School was instrumental in elevating that opponent. If Roosevelt had not lost, it would have been impossible for Lincoln to be undefeated. This loss to them helped to make their season a success.

We, therefore, by indirection share in their glory as they did when they lost to us. Of course, this is a weak attempt to exalt losing merely to prevent further embarrassment and save face.

Judge a Team on How It Looks

Every heart swells with pride in victory and those same hearts shrink a bit when failure is encountered. In my philosophy, losing is not a tragedy, but the manner in which you lose may be. Our head coach, Glenn Killinger, has taught me to judge a team not just in terms of whether it wins or loses, but how it looks in that process. Your squad should be fundamentally sound, and have the spirit of the occasion, which means wanting to kick hell out of an opponent—legally. I have been more proud of our team after they played good football, yet suffered a defeat, than when they played poorly and barely lucked one out. There is little satisfaction which accrues from the latter.

If my team is playing in its class and up to its potential I will win my share of games. On the other hand, I cringe a little when my men give a sub-par performance. A hole burns inside, and a little of me is always left on the field.

chapter ten

RELATIONSHIP WITH PLAYERS
DURING THE OFF-SEASON

A second rate man can never make a first class ball player—
J. S. WHITE

Coaching is a year 'round profession, which is never restricted to the playing season alone. A good coach, when not actually coaching, is preparing to do so.

Since it is a full-time profession without vacation, so too, the relationship involved must not have interruptions. It must continue unabated.

Relationship during the off-season is important, for it helps you to maintain a hold and check on players who are now separated from you. What players do out of season has a direct bearing on your sport, so it is necessary to keep a constant vigil. A head coach must keep uppermost in mind the many forces that reach out to entangle players between seasons. In order to combat those influences you must prepare a series of letters to be forwarded to your players at strategically planned intervals.

Make-Up of Letter

For expediency, it would be wise to write the letters sometime in April or May. Date them according to your mailing desires. Have them mimeographed; place them in envelopes; address and stamp them. Then put them away. Write a note to yourself on your home calendar reminding you when to mail them.

Call on the English Department

Writing these letters offers a fine opportunity for you to solicit the aid of the school's English teachers. It is suggested you do this whether you need help or not. This enables faculty members to share your project and gives them a feeling of belonging. Your request for their help inflates their ego and gives them a part in what you are doing. It also advertises the fact that coaching is a full time endeavor.

Another advantage is the check they provide on vocabulary, spelling, and sentence construction. Letters going out to the community should be written in impeccable English. Some people are known for their tendency to pounce on errors in English.

Follow-up Letters

A portion of your first letter to your squad members contains a request that they write you concerning their whereabouts and activities. Boys usually respond punctually; however, some may be dilatory. Here a follow-up letter is required. Insist on knowing how they are spending their time.

On the other hand, some replies may bring word which causes consternation and concern. Perhaps they are engaged in work or spending their time in a manner which you know is detrimental. You immediately write with the hope of redirecting their undertakings. If that fails to produce the desired results, a personal visit is a must. Solving problems during the summer means fewer headaches once the season gets under way.

Samples of Off-Season Letters

Every coach must establish an efficient off-season relationship, and this is most important for a beginning mentor. It is his initiation in inter-personal relationship. Coaches can succeed in accomplishing this through letters.

The following pages will present copies of letters bearing

various important messages during the off-season. Each letter is mailed with the intent of creating a state of readiness. Readiness in attitude, skill, and a willingness to work toward a team concept when the season begins, will be a direct result of these planned communications.

June 27, 1958

To: ALL FOOTBALL CANDIDATES
From: YOUR FOOTBALL COACH

This is a most dangerous time of the year, because you are not participating in your sport. We all know that you do in a game what you do in practice. Games are not won on Saturday. They are won on Monday, Tuesday, Wednesday, Thursday, and Friday. By the same token, games are not won solely during the season—they are also won during the off season.

What are you doing *now* to win next fall? Are you still training? Are you getting enough rest? Are you smoking or drinking? Are you running with a fast crowd of girls and boys? Are you hurting tomorrow's team today? Remember, today is the tomorrow you worried about yesterday. If you live a clean American life, you will never have occasion to worry.

The coaching staff wants you to have fun. They want you to have a really enjoyable summer. Good boys enjoy their summer by participating in clean, wholesome activities. Only decent boys who are used to obeying rules can play on decent teams.

If you disobey the social laws of your community, you will break training rules, and then we don't want you on our squad. We want gentlemen on and off the field. The minute you become a member of an athletic team you belong to the public. You become a missionary for your school. Everything you do is noticed and appraised.

You must stand tall to be above the crowd. Big things are asked of big people. Be big. Have the courage to say "No" to friends who want to play chicken games and run around all hours of the night. Boys who need that type of excitement are frustrated and need psychiatric treatment. Be oblivious to outside pressures.

Develop speed of mind, eye, and feet. Look alive by being alert and quick. Try to like all people and get along because you have self control.

Make visible your tact and forebearance without suffering any loss of integrity.

If you think this is trifling and unimportant—then don't come out for the squad. Remember, trifling makes perfection, and perfection is no trifle.

You, your parents, and your school will never be ashamed, because you have done your best.

My sincere and personal wishes to you for a fine healthy summer.

Yours truly,

Joe Doakes
606 Owen Road
West Chester, Pa.

Kindly drop me a line informing me of your summer doings.

Equipment Day—Aug. 30 2:30 P.M. Gym
First Practice—Sept. 3—9:30 A.M.

July 25, 1958

Memo to: VARSITY PARENTS
From: JOE DOAKES, FOOTBALL COACH

The character of a sport can be no better than the parents of the boys who play it. Because I sincerely believe that statement, I hope someday to award varsity letters not only to members of my football squad but to every parent as well. Without excellent parental cooperation, winning teams could never be realized. Our work is often made so much easier in coaching because your home training period has lightened our load. Your son reflects your strength of character and integrity.

In athletics a team relationship is necessary. The team is comprised of player, parent, and coach. This trio must work together towards achieving common objectives. Only through the harmonious blending of these efforts can success be realized. Any breakdown anywhere along the line will result in serious repercussions in the won and lost column.

We want boys on our squad who heed parental advice—who respect and obey. If they respect parents—they will respect coaches. Discipline is like a girl on a date, who gets only as much respect as she demands. I know you demand respect and obedience from your boy. No fine parent can afford to be lax in this department. You dare not sacrifice respect for popularity.

This letter is addressed to you because our success is dependent upon your thoughtful, vigilant mind. We expect you to continue to exert a profound beneficial influence on your son.

Please insist he gets to bed by 10:30 every night, excepting, of course, a minimum of special occasions. If he is too old to regard this advice with care, then he is too old for our ball club.

If he gets into a fast crowd, slow him down to a walk. If things come to a showdown insist that he make changes. Do not compromise.

Supervise his girl relationships with a definiteness that spells sound guidance. This relationship, more than any other, leads to athletic deterioration. Young boys need counselling and advice. Do not be näive in this matter. How you handle this situation will have paramount influence on his program in athletic competition.

Insist that his nights out be restricted to only the weekend. Supervise his studying. Make him study. School today is much easier than in your day. *You did it. Make him do it too.*

Remember, growing up means not doing what comes naturally and doing the things you do not like to do. Discourage your boy from buying a car. The American automobile must share major responsibility for the partial decadence of American morals. It is easy for parents to brag about their material progress because their children drive their own cars. In most instances, the car will enable him to move faster downhill. We ask you merely to postpone offering him his own car until he is older and more mature.

If he already has a car, compare his behavior now with that before the car entered his life. Can you answer this question: Where was he last night, and with whom?

Not too long ago these temptations were confronting me, and I'm grateful to my parents and coach for guiding me to choose the right path.

Winning football teams are developed not by the apparent adolescent boys who are playing the game today, but by parents who reared that team of youngsters when they were one, two, ten, twelve, and thirteen years of age.

On September 10th we will have a "TAPPON" night, and I hope you can be present. "Tappon" is an abbreviation for town officials, administrators, players, parents, game officials, and newspapermen.

Joe Doakes
Coach

Through this type of communication an ingenious method of stimulating enthusiasm results.

The Mather Letter

Charles V. Mather was one of the outstanding high school coaches whose efforts and fine organization have resulted in 11 State Championships for Massillon High School of Ohio.

While attending the Ohio Clinic I received a copy of his letter to parents, which carries a real message. It follows:

July 2, 1958

Dear Parent,

We are very happy to have your son on our 1958 football squad, I feel confident this squad has the possibilities of making just as good a record as previous squads. You note I say possibilities, as we never know how intent a squad will be toward winning a championship until November 17th. We do know that few good things in life come easily and success in any venture takes a lot of effort. Each succeeding year of championship ball becomes more difficult. It is much easier to become a champion than to stay a champion.

Football is a part of our educational system. Mr. Kemp, our very able principal, is in charge of this educational system at our school and is very much interested in the part played by athletics. We, on the football staff, naturally believe that this part of our system can play a leading role in your son's education for life. I know you are intensely interested in having your son become a fine man, and I assure you that is our keenest desire too.

We feel that three important phases in every man's life are his physical well being, moral characteristics, and mental alertness. Physically, you have endowed your son with a good sturdy body or he wouldn't be out for football. You will see born in him a new confidence and courage. When you meet and compete each day with your teammates and opponents on a physical basis, you soon acquire the confidence and courage for which all men are respected.

Morally—we encourage your son to be a gentleman at all times. There was a time when only "the toughies" were considered football players, but that time passed when fine, red-blooded men and boys found what a thrilling game football really was.

We do not at any time permit smoking, or other forms of intemperate living. Regular sleeping hours are very important to a growing boy. We hope sincerely that you will help him keep his training. We do not consider this training a sacrifice on his part, because it contributes to his physical well being.

Mentally—we can provide through football many experiences that have a direct carryover into life. I will just mention two for briefness' sake. First, accepting responsibility and carrying it through to a successful end. How can a boy be subjected to any more responsibility than carrying out his assignments before thousands of people during a season knowing that if he cannot carry out these assignments he will be replaced. Second, the will to win. We want to win every game if it can be done fairly. We want your son to have the same desire, and he must have, if our season is going to be successful. In life, he will have to be a winner if he is going to be successful. So if we can further this desire at an early age, it should help him to be a winner in his endeavors in later life.

Our team next fall will be playing the most difficult schedule a Massillon team has ever undertaken. We are counting on our team motto to pull us through; "It takes work to be good, and if we aren't good, we have no one to blame but ourselves."

If at any time we coaches can be of service to you or your son, please call on us.

Very sincerely yours,

Charles V. Mather
Athletic Director & Coach

August 5, 1958

Memo To: PLAYERS
From: COACH
Subject: CONDITION

Men, in approximately three weeks we will begin football practice. Football is a hard contact game, one that requires excellent conditioning. Not only will it be necessary to out-fundamental our opponents, but we must out-condition them too.

Pre-season practice time is no longer sufficient to cover the many aspects of today's game, plus the need to get into tip-top shape. Because of the time element, the coaches are requesting that you embark on a training schedule immediately. Walk two miles every day—if possible, run four miles daily. Do push ups, knee bends, and leg exercises every day. Cut down your swimming, as it tends to soften the skin and will result in bad feet.

Only by reporting in fine physical condition can we begin with real contact work immediately. We are too thin in number to lose men through injuries. The coaching staff is convinced that if you report with a body hardened through calisthenics, injuries will be reduced to a minimum.

You experienced men know when the going gets tough—when yards come hard—when your backs are to the goal posts, you have to be in tip-top shape to stop the score. It takes guts to get to bed early—to exercise daily—to cut down on your smoking. The coaches want only men with that kind of courage to make up our next squad.

Remember, winners never quit and quitters never win.

Will you let your teammates down, or will you contribute to your squad's success?

Will you be part of the solution or will you be part of the problem?

Please don't let us down—start to get into shape.

Coach Mitten

The following two letters are samples of those sent to candidates fifteen days before the opening of practice. The first one was sent by Head Coach Killinger to members of the 1957 West Chester State Teachers College football squad. It follows:

August 15, 1958

Dea Joe, Frank, Jim, etc.

Football practice for the 1958 season will begin on August 28, when the entire squad will meet at 8 P.M. in the Television Room, Wayne Hall. The entire coaching staff will be on hand to extend their greeting.

We had a splendid season in 1956, when we defeated seven opponents on an eight game schedule. It will be difficult to equal this record, especially in view of our schedule. However, I believe that it can be done. Baldwin-Wallace College is a newcomer to our schedule and is only slightly inferior to Youngstown University in playing ability. Fort Myer replaces Delaware and any service team is usually a difficult opponent.

The entire coaching staff is enthusiastic about our prospects for the coming season, despite the loss of almost an entire line. What our present candidates lack in size and experience will have to be made up by great enthusiasm and wonderful spirit. Frankly, our line is our major problem. Practically all of our backs from 1956 will return and last year they did a splendid job. It is possible that one or more Sophomores may develop into starting backs.

As Head Coach, it will be my pleasure to welcome you on August 28. You will be quartered in Wayne Hall and eat in the College Dining Room. It has always been my contention that a football team which displays great determination, hustle, and intelligence will be a winning team. I EXPECT EACH MEMBER OF THE VARSITY SQUAD TO CONTRIBUTE JUST A LITTLE MORE THAN HIS ABILITY INDICATES—THAT IS THE TRUE TEST OF A CHAMPION.

Lots of luck and I will expect to hear from you by return mail, acknowledging receipt of this letter, and advising me that you will report on August 28th.

Sincerely yours,

W. Glenn Killinger,
Head Coach of Football

The following letter is a sample of one which may be sent to high school candidates.

August 15, 1958

Dear Joe, Jim, Frank, etc.

From Bunker Hill to Pearl Harbor, our forefathers were driven by a burning desire to win. Winning was a passion to them. No one is ever happy to come in second.

The man who loses learns to lose gracefully; nevertheless he continues to covet victory—even more.

Stories coming from Pearl Harbor tell us that our men manned the guns until the intense heat buckled the decks right under them. They didn't know the meaning of "quit" or "surrender" even in the face of insurmountable odds.

The coaches want men to report for practice with that spirit and attitude. We want men who promise to do their best at all times.

On Wednesday, August 28, at 10 A.M., you are to receive your football equipment. This will enable our supply manager to order new gear for men whose old outfits no longer fit them.

Come out with the attitude you will make the starting eleven. I promise you the entire coaching staff will work with you so you may realize your desire. Good Luck and God Bless You.

Coach Bonder

A SUMMONS

A Summons

The following letter is used to summon your squad for practice.

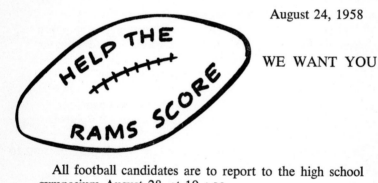

August 24, 1958

WE WANT YOU

All football candidates are to report to the high school gymnasium August 28, at 10 A.M.

IMPORTANT

IMPORTANT

PLEASE READ CAREFULLY

RETURN THE ENCLOSED PARENTAL PERMISSION CARD IMMEDIATELY IF YOU INTEND TO TRY OUT FOR FOOTBALL.

1. DR. KISTLER WILL EXAMINE ALL CANDIDATES AT THIS TIME.

2. NO ONE WILL BE PERMITTED TO PRACTICE UNTIL HE HAS HAD A MEDICAL EXAMINATION AND RETURNED HIS PARENTAL PERMISSION CARD.
3. THE FIRST FORMAL PRACTICE WILL START AT 10 A.M. SHARP, SEPTEMBER 3-4-5-6-7.
4. WE WILL PRACTICE TWICE A DAY AT 10 A.M. AND AT 2 P.M. RAIN OR SHINE.
5. MAKE ARRANGEMENTS TO BE ON HAND FOR ALL PRACTICE SESSIONS. IF YOU ARE INJURED COME OUT AND OBSERVE IF AT ALL POSSIBLE.
6. FIRST GAME, SEPTEMBER 20 AT RADNOR HIGH SCHOOL.
　　　WE MUST—WE WILL BE READY

Coach Brennen

Through the use of these planned messages your boys will never lose sight of their game.

Counting Noses Through Parental Permission Cards

The return of the parental permission cards will reveal the identity of the returning candidates. This provides a basis for definitive planning.

If one of your bread and butter aspirants has decided to give up the game for one reason or another, you will have time to alter your seasonal plans. You can accomplish this change long before the initial workout takes place.

Youngsters dislike changing their positions after practice gets under way. Setting them up before practice starts by laying the necessary ground work and keeps the relationship on an even keel.

Presenting the Squad

It is wise to have a meeting in order to present your squad to the town, administrators, parents, officials, and newspapermen. This organization should be given a nick-name which is catching and conveys a message. The name "Tappon" is suggested.

Invitations in the form of letters to those people must be sent out at least four days before the meeting. It would be prudent if you asked a well-known district figure to act as toastmaster. Invite the head of every neighborhood organization to attend, and if possible, to say a few words. This builds up fine community morale. Do not neglect to introduce your administrators and school board president. Try to avoid slighting anyone and apologize at the outset for the possibility that you may do so unintentionally.

Have the squad dressed in game equipment and run a few basic plays. Take time to explain the intricacies of your system. Introduce your entire squad and say something nice about each boy.

The meeting should terminate with refreshments being served. The fathers of the members of your squad could handle this phase of the program.

A sample of the invitation letter follows.

TAPPON—SUMMONS—YOU

September 6, 1958

Dear Friend,

The 1958 football contingent of Western High School will be happy to have you meet them Thursday, September 10th, in the high school gymnasium at 8:30 P.M.

For the past two weeks we have been practicing diligently to give the community a representative team. We are most eager that you meet us, our coaches, and school officials.

The team will be dressed in game uniform ready to run off some of its basic plays in order to present you with a sampling of its offensive maneuvers.

We anticipate a representation of every organization in the district to honor us with their presence. Town officials, administrators, game officials, players, parents, and newspapermen will be present.

May we please count on your presence?

Yours truly,

The Squad

MEND YOUR FENCES

Improve Your Knowledge

After communications to your squad are fully planned, you can turn your attention to other important areas.

The summer is the time for you to evaluate and take inventory. If you feel there is some phase of the game in which you have a pronounced weakness, take steps to overcome it. Make your weaknesses your strongest assets. In so doing you will make your squad richer. They will receive more efficient and more comprehensive coaching.

Visit successful college coaches and ask them to help you. They will not refuse aid, especially to a young man venturing on an initial coaching experience.

Mend the Breach

If you have alienated the friendship of some faculty member or administrator during the year, seek him out and mend the breach. Apologize sincerely and resolve never to repeat the offense. In coaching, you must keep your enemies at a minimum.

Oftentimes we antagonize some member of the community. Perhaps it is a parent. Action must be taken to wipe out all misunderstanding and replace it with a new harmonious relationship.

In attempting to restore good working conditions, be humble and assume sole responsibility for creating the unpleasantness. That assumption will make the peacemaking much easier than it would be if you defend your position.

Taking these steps during the summer insures a beginning with a clean slate in relationship, thus enabling you to devote full time to your coaching chores.

chapter eleven

POSTSCRIPT

Coach—"The Man"

It is characteristic of small men to avoid challenges, of big men to meet them——CHARLES KINGSLEY

Because the preceding pages are replete with numerous techniques, varied duties, and pressing responsibilities to be assumed by a coach in establishing an acceptable functioning relationship, it is prudent to look at the coach as *a man*.

Someone once remarked that there are two types of men inhabiting this planet. There are men with a small "m" and men with a capital "M." The coaching profession is a tremendous undertaking constantly calling for man's best efforts, therefore, he must fit the category of a man with a capital "M."

The Good and Bad of a Pedestal

The author regrets the need to write the following paragraph, because its contents present an enigma. Truth, however, must not give way to maudlin sentimentality. It cannot be concealed by hiding evidence of its existence.

Some coaches today enjoy more prestige than administrators and teachers. Most coaches today stand on a pedestal. I am in complete agreement with readers who rebel over the existence of this embarrassing situation. That it is an actuality, however, is important. Inquire the identity of an outstanding teacher, principal or department head. Ask anyone at random to name the presidents of our ten leading universities, and a blank stare will be fixed on the questioner. Request the name of an outstanding player or the coach of those same institutions, and presto! you have them. Perhaps the fine contribution of an educational institution is taken for granted. Perhaps the emphasis by public relationists is in the wrong field, but facts must be honored. As a teacher, I envy the success and limelight in which coaches bask. I covet their stature and bigger dimensions. At a recent meeting I overheard a teacher remark, "If only I could engender the enthusiasm for learning that Coach Brill generates with his football team, I could be the Grand Panjandrum himself, and solve my motivational problems." Coach Brill might have answered, "Enthusiasm is caught, not taught."

Because the public has placed coaches on a pedestal, it is binding on the coaching profession to approve for membership only men of good character. The first requisite is that he be a good man. *We do what we are—We are what we do.*

No Two Alike

Coaching demands a constant change in your attitude toward players, which eliminates the listing of any static qualities. Given a normal complement of players, you must adapt your personality to deal with the individual eccentricities of each man. No two individuals are ever alike in all respects. No two fingerprints and no two personalities are ever the same. The little girl was profoundly wise who said: "When God made rabbits, he said 'Let there be rabbits,' and there were rabbits. But when God made babies, he made them one by one."

You are, therefore, confronted with wide differences among your players.. These differences are in physique, personality, background, education and experiences. In utilizing the techniques that appear on the previous pages, adjust these differences to meet your individual situation.

The Coaching Personality

Psychologists have defined personality as one's reaction to a social setting. As the social setting, emotional climate, and time element are forever changing, a constant personality is an impossibility.

First and foremost, you must be a good teacher. Good coaching is good teaching transferred from the classroom to the playing field. Some writers have attempted to list necessary attributes, such as, dynamic, inspiring, fearless, cold, overt, relaxed, meticulous, sympathetic, understanding, cruel, hard, companionable, and possessing unsurpassed determination; he must radiate warmth, and his frankness must at times be frightening. The list is endless. Every coach has some of these qualities by nature, and the others must be cultivated. It is hardly necessary to write that the more of the aforementioned qualities you possess, the more tools are at your command to do the job.

THE TWELVE QUALIFICATIONS OF A COMPETENT COACH

1. He must be a man of good character, who wants to be a leader of a strong team. He selects able and imaginative co-workers. In order to infuse a team concept within his group, he must emerge with absolute power and dominate them without difficulty. Because of this kinship, he prepares to stand alone to face criticism directed either at him or at any of his charges. He protects people working for him, for they must never appear in a bad light. In other words, he carries out the principle. *"Loyalty down the line as well as up the line."*

2. Despite his strong arm, he must encourage independent thought on the part of his subordinates. The important factor is making provisions for them to divulge their new ideas in a manner which will not be a threat to his authority. Special meetings are convened in which coaches utilize their authority to encourage the cooperation of assistants in making contributions.

3. He must never use his authority to abuse his charges. He remembers that his command is delegated to him by the players.

It is his exercise only if he makes use of it to help them. He must believe in human dignity as a basic quality of man. To accomplish this, it is vital to treat players not only for what they are, but for what they might become. In this manner, deep respect for the coach not only emerges, but also solidifies.

4. His feelings must range from paternalism to scorn for those with whom he deals in order to achieve results. The exercise of these emotions must be consistent so that no favoritism occurs. It is necessary to humble and praise men as the occasion warrants. The application of these sentiments is readily accepted by players as a portion of their fate. Fear of castigation and desire for acclaim offer ample stimulation to effort. The *have nots* always want what the *have's* have—namely, commendation.

5. Because of his absolute power, he can and must delegate to his assistants as much routine as possible, for he must assume that they can carry out their duties. Keeping them happy by extolling their contributions cements his top position. It is wise to solicit their cooperation in making decisions. Should these decisions backfire, he alone takes the blame. If they succeed, he shares the glory.

6. He must feel he possesses the ultimate right to try, judge, and punish anyone whose interests conflict with those needed for team success. Conversely, he must be consistent and do exactly what he expects others to do. He cannot formulate policies which will hurt his subordinates. A feeling of harmony can be realized if this becomes a uniform policy.

7. He expects all to give beyond the call of duty, if only for the reason that he will do the same.

8. He respects his supervisors and avoids hostility—he never starts in the middle and works both sides. He gives to his superiors whatever he has asked from his subordinates.

9. He must see that every player is assigned a responsibility in which he has aptitude and will excel. Never embarrass a player by seeking the impossible. It is better to be a leader, not a "boss." Orders are the connecting link between the coach and the team. They determine whether he is a real leader or a driver. Players yearn for effective leadership; this develops a situation in which

they are driven but are unconscious to the force. They resent an overt domination. Coaches camouflage their authority by dressing up their command with a convincing finesse. Direction must be tailored to suit both the individual and the situation.

10. Coaches and players together punish themselves to achieve not for selfish motives, but to be of service to the community's continued growth. As the community flourishes, the prestige of the coach increases proportionately.

11. The coach must obtain personal satisfaction from seeing players develop and grow academically as well as athletically.

12. Once a policy has been established and agreed upon, it is the coach's duty to hold every player responsible for its implementation.

INVASION

Operation "Take Over"

Some years ago, Orson Welles dramatized on the radio the invasion of earth by men from outer space. His performance was organized in such a way that listeners did not realize it was a radio show and were convinced of the authenticity of the attack. The wires leading to police and authorities hummed. Telephone operators were frantic because of the calls. As Welles located the invasion point near Trenton, New Jersey, the Governor was summoned and the State Police and Militia were alerted. Confusion reigned until the authorities traced the attack to Station, "WJZ," from which Welles' outstanding ingenuity had paralyzed the entire eastern seaboard with fear. The confusion was heightened by the need to cancel scheduled programs in order to assure the public that the attack was merely a radio story with no foundation in fact. It was all a hoax.

The following however, is no hoax. It is true. An invasion is starting by a huge, powerful army so vast, so enormous, so gigantic that no force on the earth, not even atomic weapons, can prevent it. Even our secret armaments are rendered sterile. The attack has already begun. It is under way at this very moment. Its advance cannot be delayed. This new host will invade the Senate and the House of Representatives and force them out. The President of the United States will have to go, along with the Vice President, the Cabinet, and every government worker in Washington, D.C. There will be no compromise, no peace, not even "unconditional surrender." The Pentagon will change. Our local mayor, the governor and entire state structure will be cast aside. Nothing can conquer this force. It is a phenomenon. Modern America, with its intricate scientific knowledge, cannot stem the tide of this new invader. Further to insure the conquest, even our new weapons will be taken over by this unconquerable array. Our homes will fall to them, and our school administrators and teachers will be replaced.

This aggregation is destined to become America's greatest asset because it consists of our present generation. They will be tomorrow's parents, presidents, governors, mayors, teachers, doctors and scientists. Nothing can stop the transition.

As a coach, you must play your part in preparing this group for the eventual invasion. What you contribute will be in evidence throughout posterity. Proper leadership must be furnished to them. Along with guided missiles, there must be guided morals, so that when "D-Day" arrives, America will be stronger and greater because of your efforts.

Whatever this new army is—it is no more than what you helped make it. What the present invasion accomplishes today will be remembered for a million tomorrows.

INDEX

Winning (*cont.*)
  through planning, 41-42
    fooling opponent, 133-134
    outmaneuvering opponent, 134-135
    surprising opponent, 135
  turnstiles, 120-121
  public reaction, 141
    envy, 141
    rumor, 141
    suspicion, 141

Winning relationship, 117-144
Wolf, Dick, 33

Y

"Yes" men, 41
Yohe, Jack, 136
Young, Cy, 159
Youngstown University, 33, 70, 132

Z

Zero, 65

B